The
Turning Wheel

The
Turning Wheel

A Study of Contracts and Oaths in Wagner's *Ring*

David A. White

Selinsgrove: Susquehanna University Press
London and Toronto: Associated University Presses

© 1988 by Associated University Presses, Inc.

Associated University Presses
440 Forsgate Drive
Cranbury, NJ 08512

Associated University Presses
25 Sicilian Avenue
London WC1A 2QH, England

Associated University Presses
P.O. Box 488, Port Credit
Mississauga, Ontario
Canada L5G 4M2

The paper used in this publication meets the requirements
of the American National Standard for Permanence of Paper
for Printed Library Materials Z39.48-1984.

Library of Congress Cataloging-in-Publication Data

White, David A., 1942–
  The turning wheel.

  Bibliography: p.
  Includes index.
  1. Wagner, Richard, 1813–1883.   Ring des Nibelungen.
I. Title.
ML410.W15W19   1988   782.1′092′4   87-42795
ISBN 0-941664-89-9 (alk. paper)

Printed in the United States of America

To Francis D. Lazenby

To be entangled with those mouth-made vows,
Which break themselves in swearing!

—*Antony and Cleopatra,* 1.3

Contents

Preface

There are many books on Wagner and many books on Wagner's *Der Ring des Nibelungen*. Some books on the *Ring* are long, others are short. A short book on the *Ring* has a distinct advantage over a long book on the *Ring*—the reader may finish it quickly and then return to the *Ring* proper, either by studying the music and libretto, by listening to it on recordings, or, should one's zeal be pitched high, by attending the next Bayreuth festival. On the assumption that the short book has something to offer, the student of Wagner will, after reading it, return to the *Ring* with enhanced vision of its seemingly endless riches. And if the book is something less than successful, then brevity becomes a virtue.

The purpose of this short study is straightforward. I have selected a single narrative element—contracts and oaths (as a type of contract)—and traced its development throughout the *Ring*. Although the interplay joining contracts and oaths with individual characters originates and is focused on Wotan, it rapidly radiates to the outermost reaches of the *Ring*'s symbolic universe. Wagner carefully establishes this universality by having Wotan, king of the gods and guardian of the world, become contractually involved with the other gods, giants, men, dwarves, and various anthropomorphic embodiments of nature—in short, with representatives of all levels of the *Ring*'s cosmological structure. Furthermore, the audience learns about the increasing and ultimately definitive importance of these contracts and oaths from Wotan himself via monologues, conversations Wotan has with other characters, and discussions about Wotan when he himself is absent from the dramatic action. Even from a purely aesthetic perspective, quite apart from its obvious role in the thought-structure of the libretto, the contract as an institution is just as important to the *Ring* as are the characters linked to each other by that institution.

The analysis offered in chapter 2 of this pivotal institution is not sequential in the sense that the episodes discussed follow the actual dramatic course of events in the *Ring*. But the analysis is sequential in that it is based on a comprehensive understanding of the *Ring*, from which perspective the structure of contracts can be systematically presented. Thus, I have assumed that all the events of the *Ring* are at hand, spread across a horizon on which all relevant points are visible. This perspective allows more freedom in, for example, connecting an event occurring in *Das Rheingold* with its cause as stated in some other music drama. As we shall see, such interpretive freedom is necessary in order to determine the dramatic and philosophical significance of this particularly pervasive element in the *Ring's* structure. Texts from Wagner's poem for the *Ring* are cited throughout this study; their arrangement and connection are intended to demonstrate the function and implications of contracts as one complex part within an even more complex whole. It should go without saying that if the *Ring* is as great a work of art as I and many others believe, it would be presumptuous in the extreme to offer an interpretation that attempted to explain in detail all the principal elements in its symbolic universe. The following interpretation is intended to be comprehensive only in light of that one element that serves as the controlling motif.

Although some of the commentary in this study is necessarily somewhat abstract, thus mirroring the philosophical content of its subject, I have tempered this abstraction by considering the ramifications of crucial contracts and oaths for other elements of the *Ring* that are either related or tangent to these contracts and oaths. The motivations and emotional aspects of characters as they enter into or attempt to fulfill contracts and the subtle but carefully considered ways in which Wagner has integrated elements of nature—for instance, wood and water—with the institution of contracts are perhaps the most prominent examples of this subsidiary commentary. In this way, the global presence of contracts in the *Ring* should become more apparent, especially in places where that presence is not immediately discernible.

The study is in three parts. Chapter 1 is an examination of several important critical attitudes and positions toward the *Ring* insofar as they bear on the possibility of an interpretation of the sort I wish to advance. Such a preamble is, I feel, an essential critical exercise, given what will be for some students of Wagner the apparent dryness of the notion of contracts in addition to the prevailing view among Wagnerians that Wagner was something less than a master of abstract thought. Chapter 2 is the account of the function of contracts in the *Ring*. It is subdivided into three sections: Contracts and the Origin of Power, Contracts and the Preservation of Power, Contracts and the Loss of Power. This subdivision will allow the full scope of contracts and oaths to be developed, in particular with respect to power and, more generally, with respect to numerous other fundamental elements in the *Ring*. Chapter 3 is an epilogue consisting of a retrospective discussion of the post-Götterdämmerung world. In addition to considering the status of contracts, this retrospect will branch off into brief analyses of the nature and relative importance of values such as power, wisdom, freedom, and love. It should be noted that, although grounded in the letter of the *Ring*, this retrospect is speculative in content. But since Wagner intended the *Ring* to be philosophically penetrating as well as aesthetically persuasive, we do no disservice either to philosophy or to Wagner by honoring this intention, at least to a certain point. The reader should perhaps be advised at the outset, however, that in this commentary I attempt to steer a middle course between the rigors of political philosophy on the one hand and an inappropriately abstract and rigidified imposition on the glorious orchestral and vocal swells of the *Ring* on the other. Thus, definitive answers to the questions raised in this chapter will not appear and should not be expected. But some initial steps in search of these answers can only sharpen our awareness of the *Ring* as an attempt to express one man's vision of the truth through the vibrant medium of operatic art.

Acknowledgments

I wish to thank Mary Jeanne Larrabee for her editorial efforts and for her labors during our pilgrimage to Bayreuth. And I must also thank Marie White for her labor in preparing the manuscript.

The
Turning Wheel

1

The Wagnerian Libretto: Principles of Interpretation

The serious student of Wagner's *Der Ring des Nibelungen* may be serious to the point of aspiring to become a "perfect Wagnerite." Such a student will then be faced with a difficult problem, the solution to which is even more complex than that offered by the first Wagnerian to proclaim the possibility of such perfection, George Bernard Shaw. The perfect Wagnerite would have perfect comprehension and appreciation of the music, the libretto (including the staging), and the panorama of relations between the two. The scope of this panorama is enormous, the interplay between sound and word touching on many fundamental features of the human drama. The immediate focus for the resolution of the Wagnerian version of that drama is doubtless the cast of characters—ranging hierarchically from scheming deities to oafish giants and knavish dwarves—all interlocking in their respective personal and ultimately human quest for the Rhinegold. A perfect union between the spectator and a work of this magnitude will be measured by the extent to which the spectator can feel and think his way into the motivations and actions of these characters. But such penetration is only the first step in a critical undertaking that requires a large number of different interpretive attitudes.

To affirm that the perfect Wagnerite must think as well as feel implies that the *Ring* itself contains thought of some form. For if the *Ring* were not thoughtful, then perfection would consist in little more than a bacchic fusion between spectator and aural content of the music and that secondary "thought" advanced through its leitmotifs. The music of the *Ring* is undoubtedly thoughtful in this sense. Wagner's genius at creating the most exquisitely subtle musical relationships among leitmotifs representing vastly different types of reality is a source of continuous revelation. But the poem which serves as the basis for the *Ring*'s libretto is equally rich and equally worthy of careful consideration. And the nature of this poem is such that, regardless of the extent of one's own emotional reaction to the pure sound of the music, the aspirant to Wagnerian perfection must *think* the poem through before these emotions can be given proper direction. Furthermore, the process of thinking the poem through does not culminate in just the exact knowledge of which individual character is doing what to whom and why. The "why" must consider not only the interpersonal dimension of the characters taken individually (a dimension duly complex), but also the more universal social and ethical dimension that underlies their individual actions. This second dimension is essential to the structure of the *Ring*. Although its presence is not always explicitly felt as the dramatic action unfolds, the social and ethical dimension becomes crucial for determining the significance of all the more immediate interpersonal conflicts. If the *Ring* is intended to be cathartic in a moral and social sense—and not merely "great art," then problems concerning its more abstract content are not mere critical improvisation and festoonery. The more one knows about the thoughtful content of the *Ring*, the closer one approaches the ideals serving to guide the perfect Wagnerite toward his goal.

The purpose of this study is to examine Wagner's poem for the *Ring* in order to develop one specific aspect of the *Ring's* underlying social and ethical dimension. But before that project can be initiated, two relevant objections must be considered, objections that are directed at the very possibility of such a project. The first objection may be stated thus: The *Ring* as a work of art is an organic unity. To separate the poem as libretto from the music is to disrupt that unity, perhaps to the point of negating whatever insights may appear when the poem is approached in such abstract isolation. The second objection, closely related to the first, is that even if the integrity of the work were not destroyed after the heuristic separation of poem from music, the poem thus separated fails to stand on its own, both aesthetically and philosophically. The poem of the *Ring* is, according to some, both inferior as poetry and inferior as philosophy. Therefore, even if the intended distinction between poem and music is not aesthetically disruptive, the results of the distinction remain useless, even as a heuristic gambit.

For several leading authorities on Wagner and his operas, objections of this sort follow naturally from what are, for these authorities, certain sound though unstated critical principles. But these principles contain presuppositions which should be brought into the open and examined. In this case, a critical discussion of these objections and their underlying principles will lead into a general formulation of the presuppositions which ground the interpretive focus of this study. My belief is that any interpretation of a work with the awesome magnitude of the *Ring* may stand or fall by the strength or weakness of the principles which serve as the basis for that interpretation.

Consider now the first objection, implicit in this remark about Wotan. The eminent Wagnerian Ernest Newman says that "Wotan must stand or fall by his own dramatic grandeur and by the quality of the music that is given to him to sing, not by the degree of success with which he illustrates a particular theory of the Will."[1] The "theory of the Will" is, of course, a reference to Schopenhauer and his influence on Wagner's own thinking. Newman's point can be generalized as follows: Regardless of what philosophical notion may be allied with Wotan, the quality of his music and his stature as a dramatic character determine his significance in the *Ring*. However, the validity of this position depends on yet another generalization of even wider scope, namely that the artistic value of the *Ring* is based solely on the music and the "dramatic grandeur" (or whatever dramatic value is appropriate for Fafner, Fricka, Mime, Brünnhilde, etc.) of those parts of the poem which, in conjunction with the music, collectively establish these values. Thus, the musical embodiment of the *Ring*'s poem is a necessary factor in appreciating the *Ring* as an artistic whole. To separate the poem from the music in search of the ideas expressed in the poem for the music will destroy the *Ring* as a work of art. Wotan's significance as a dramatic character in the *Ring* is impossible to determine unless his purely musical characterization is considered in conjunction with the words he speaks.

The purpose of Newman's remark is to demonstrate that Wotan's success or failure as a character will depend on the presence or absence of aesthetic qualities, for example, "dramatic grandeur." In this sense, the point is well taken. For regardless which philosophical notion or theory Wotan was intended to exemplify, what he says and what he sings will determine whether or not Wotan succeeds aesthetically. When one actually experiences Wotan as a character, one sees a ruler who sings what he has to say. Thus, viewed solely from the perspective of performance as such, an investigation of the content of what Wotan says is obviously a derivative exercise. But of course it is no more derivative than any study of the *Ring* that attempts to interpret the meaning of what has been said by any or all characters in the *Ring*'s poem.

My principal objection to the tone if not to the letter of Newman's pronouncement is that it suggests that the thought-content Wotan represents is irrelevant for establishing Wotan's aesthetic value, i.e., that Wotan's "dramatic grandeur" is somehow independent of whatever philosophical position he may be taken to represent. And surely this is not the case. One must, at this juncture, distinguish between two different but related kinds of truth; for the sake of brevity, I shall label them philosophical truth—the truth which pertains to the world as a whole, and aesthetic truth—that peculiar truth found in the world of art. In light of this distinction, Wotan may be representative of (*a*) a thoughtful position that purports to be philosophically true or (*b*) a thoughtful position that, although it may or may not be philosophically true, is nonetheless essential in order to situate accurately Wotan's aesthetic quality *within* the dramatic action of the *Ring* as an unique aesthetic universe. One may study Wotan according to the demands of (a) and reject the position he represents as unrealistic, or as realistic but false, regardless of which philosopher inspired that position. But surely it is necessary to study Wotan's position by taking (b) into account simply in order to guarantee a sound aesthetic judgment concerning Wotan's place in the more inclusive aesthetic whole. For this purpose, the strictly philosophical content proper to Wotan's aesthetic position may be true, false, or it may simply be wildly fantastic. The only relevant aesthetic condition is that the truth of Wotan's position must be plausibly integrated with the other complex parts of the *Ring*'s dramatic structure. Newman seems to think that if Wotan represents a philosophical notion or position that is suspect or even demonstrably false, it necessarily follows that Wotan's aesthetic qualities have been marred or destroyed completely. But this conclusion is far too drastic. The philosophy underlying a dramatic figure need not be true in order for that philosophy to be aesthetically necessary.

My purpose here is not to promulgate an artificial dichotomy between art and life. The distinction between philosophical truth and aesthetic truth that I have just sketched is intended to establish some kind of distance between art and life, especially in cases such as the present, where the art in question is so penetrating and universal in scope that understanding it may become indistinguishable from understanding life in its full complexity. But I take it as axiomatic that art, however complex, is never as complex as life, and therefore that it is essential to keep the two distinct (granting that the precise line of demarcation is frequently difficult to locate). Nevertheless, it remains true that art can never be completely severed from life. Therefore, to complement the relative abstractness of this distinction, chapter 3 will reconsider the principal implications of the institution of contracts as elicited in chapter 2. In this way, it should be possible both to derive a relatively objective understanding of the *Ring* as a work of art (chapter 2) and to situate that understanding within the demands of the world of real life (chapter 3).

My argument has been that the poem of the *Ring* should be subjected to such thoughtful scrutiny before a sound aesthetic judgment can be made concerning any single moment in the *Ring* as an operatic whole. This conclusion may be developed to answer a related problem in interpretation. In cases where the precise meaning of a given passage is open to divergent interpretations (and there are many such in the *Ring*), one may wonder how to determine whether the poem or the music is the more decisive source of information. According to Wagner's *Opern und Drama*, the orchestra serves a triple function in a music drama: it has an organic relation to gesture, it occasions the remembrance of a thought or emotion, and it can give a foreboding of words yet unspoken.[2] These three functions are distinct from one another, but they share a common ground: whatever the reaction may be in the spectator, that reaction is instigated by and expressed in and through music, i.e., a purely aural medium. Thus, whatever meaning is ascribed to the musical part of the problematical passage must be determined from within that aural medium. But to verbalize the "meaning" of a musical leitmotif is to transform the music from its reality as pure sound to a verbal experience, a much different kind of reality. Musical experience can, of course, be discussed legitimately in a non-musical medium. The point is that when people argue about the meaning of a given leitmotif as found in a given operatic passage, they do not argue about the music *per se* but rather about the music to the extent that it can be translated into non-musical and discursive language. A dispute concerning the meaning of an operatic passage is not resolved by composing "refutational" music, but by demonstrating that the language expressing one alternative in the dispute is less persuasive than the language expressing another alternative.

If the Wagnerian leitmotif is as rich with possible significance as the text of the poem that is coincident with that leitmotif, it may appear that music and words are always of equal importance. This equality is, of course, essential to a full experience and understanding of the work as such. But I suggest that the equality between music and words must be set aside in certain circumstances. The primary case in point occurs when one attempts to resolve a dispute concerning the meaning of any one part of a music drama (or, indeed, the meaning of the *Ring* as a whole). As noted, the meaning of the music can be stated only if it is possible to translate musical sound into words. But since the poem as a set of unified words in effect directs the music, then the meaning of a given operatic segment depends on the relation between that segment and the meaning of the language to which the purely musical component is attached. Thus, I suggest that regardless of how potently the music of a given passage is experienced, the power and meaning of the passage as such must, in the final analysis, be related to and determined by the words that that music has animated. This is by no means to assert that the language of the poem is more receptive to precise interpretation and the ready resolution of disputes than its correlative music. The enormous volume of secondary studies of the *Ring* proves that its poetical language suggests many frequently divergent interpretations. But it is to say that the poem must serve as the more definitive source for whatever interpretations are assigned to the *Ring* as an operatic whole.

To illustrate the force of this conclusion, consider an example, one among many and one especially relevant to the purpose of this study. In scene 4 of *Das Rheingold*, Wotan is ready to seize the ring from Alberich's finger. Alberich protests loudly against the unrighteousness of this deed, but Wotan responds as follows:

Her den Ring!
Kein Recht an ihm
schwörst dein Schwatzen dir zu.

> (Give the ring here!
> Prattling so, you can swear
> no right to it.)[3]

After Wotan takes the ring, Alberich responds with the curse which sets in motion the events leading to the ultimate demise of Wotan and the old order. During Wotan's response just cited, the leitmotif representing contracts (*Verträge*) is heard in the orchestra.[4] The connection between this leitmotif and what Wotan has said is important, but its precise meaning is not immediately evident. Here are two quite distinct interpretations: (*a*) If the musical reference to contracts is related to Alberich's original theft of the gold from which the ring was forged, then the meaning of the passage as a whole could be that Alberich would have a right to the ring (a possibility which Wotan explicitly denies), had he gained the ring by contract; as things stand, however, not Alberich but Wotan has the ring by right, i.e., by right of conquest; (*b*) but if the musical reference to contracts is related to Wotan's acquisition of the ring from Alberich, then the meaning could be that neither Alberich nor Wotan has any right to the ring for the simple reason that each had to steal it—Alberich from the Rhinemaidens, Wotan from Alberich. Given these alternative interpretations, the passage as a whole becomes important as a locus for determining the meaning of right (*Recht*) in relation to the institution of contracts and in conjunction with the appropriate leitmotif. However, since the music for this passage represents *only* the institution of contracts, independent of any relation to other characters or other notions, the more adequate interpretation will emerge from looking at what Wotan has said here in conjunction with whatever other texts in the poem may be relevant for resolving this particular dispute. The answer to this or to any other interpretive problem may never be secured with any degree of certainty. The point is, however, that the leitmotif as a constitutive element in the passage as a whole cannot by itself yield the answer to the problem unless the words connected to the leitmotif are related to whatever other texts in the poem generate a relevant, ultimately discursive response.

My reply to the first objection is now complete. The second objection, which contends that the *Ring* poem is both inferior poetry and inferior philosophy, may now be addressed. Consider the poetic aspect of this objection first. In his early essay, *"Richard Wagner in Bayreuth,"* Nietzsche proposes that no one considering the status of Wagner as a poet should forget that "none of the Wagnerian dramas were intended to be read."[5] Therefore, Nietzsche adds, critical demands appropriate for literary dramas in the usual sense are inappropriate for Wagner's works. But Thomas Mann does not hesitate to invoke precisely those critical evaluations which Nietzsche has deemed inappropriate. In his essay, "The Sufferings and Greatness of Richard Wagner," Mann says that "purely as composition," the *Ring* "is often bombastic, baroque, even childish; it has something majestically and sovereignly inept-side by side with such passages of absolute genius, power, compression, primeval beauty, as disarm all doubt. . . ."[6] In sum, Mann ranges from the sharply critical to the humbly laudatory in his estimation of the work as a literary vehicle. But, according to Nietzsche, it is a mistake to think of the *Ring* in any of the critical terms proper to literary forms, as Mann apparently has just done, for the obvious reason that the poetry of the *Ring* is a libretto and not intended to stand alone as "pure" literature.

Nietzsche's critical contention is logically prior to Mann's evaluations. In other words, the very possibility of arguing with any or all of Mann's value judgments is based on proving that Nietzsche's claim is untenable. If Nietzsche's claim is true, then Mann and anyone choosing to make such literary value judgments applies criteria to part of a whole, which part by its very nature cannot be evaluated through such criteria. Nietzsche may be correct in maintaining that Wagnerian music dramas and non-operatic literary dramas are different genres and that the critical categories proper to evaluating the latter do not apply to the literary features of the former. But it does not follow that evaluation of operatic librettos as a literary genre is impossible. All one must show is that the libretto form is different from the form of other literary dramas, but at the same time is unique and independent *as a literary form*. Once the libretto assumes this independence and uniqueness, such evaluative judgments are perfectly feasible. And, in fact, there is little hesitation in making critical judgments about the purely literary quality of Shakespeare's plays without taking into account the differences between a soliloquy read in silence, read aloud, or delivered in the play as such. If literary evaluations of libretti are disallowed because libretti are intended to be sung and not read, then literary evaluations of plays should also be disallowed, since plays are intended to be acted and not read. But if the play can be established as a unique literary form, then surely the libretto can also be so established. Mann's various critical categories could then still apply to the *Ring* (although other categories may ultimately be more fitting), as long as they are based on the structure of the libretto as a unique literary form rather than on the structure of a similar but still distinct literary form. One suspects that Mann himself would reject the need for such a distinction and simply continue to press for the general reliability of his unabashedly literary judgments. But Nietzsche's point is crucial, it seems to me, and must be given due consideration before judgments of the Mann variety are accepted as relevant, much less accepted as true.

However, the point that must be made in the context of this study does not concern the soundness of given critical assessments (Mann) nor the more fundamental problem of whether such assessments are even possible (Nietzsche). It is that both Nietzsche and Mann are approaching the libretto from a primarily aesthetic perspective. As a result, the boundaries of this perspective limit the avenues open for understanding the poem. One of these avenues is based on the assumption, which I shall adopt, that the poem may be construed as a vehicle of thought at the same time that it is an aesthetic object. In other words, one may dispute what type of literary form categorizes Wagner's *Ring* libretto (or, indeed, any libretto) or, more fundamentally, one may dispute whether the libretto can be separated from the music that animates it and retain any claim to being considered a "literary" vehicle in the first place. But can one deny that however these aesthetic questions are resolved, the libretto remains intact as an ordered sequence of language representing a certain thought-content? Surely not. The thought-content may be farcical or fantastic, as many libretti are, but a libretto is no less thoughtful for being farcical. My conclusion is that determining (*a*) whether the libretto is literary and (*b*) whether the libretto, if literary, is good or bad literature is in both cases an exercise in critical aesthetics and, as such, far from unimportant. Nevertheless, it is perfectly possible to consider the libretto from a non-aesthetic perspective. The libretto then becomes an expression of thought constructed to represent a certain point of view or position that the author of the libretto deems appropriate for this particular linguistic form.

As just stated, this critical perspective might suggest that libretti are, on the whole, vehicles of noble and thoughtful sentiment. And this, of course, is not true. But some libretti are of such sentiment and, in the case of the *Ring*, something far more. For the *Ring* presents a comprehensive picture of a world doomed and another world reborn, doing so with such power that the spectator is compelled to wonder whether such is the way of that much more complex world outside the Bayreuth *Festspielhaus*. At this point, one confronts the second phase of the second objection. This phase of the objection maintains that the poem for the *Ring* is inferior philosophy and thus cannot be taken seriously from that particular standpoint, if at all. Here again is Ernest Newman:

> I do not propose to discuss the philosophical—or pseudo-philosophical—ideas of any of these works. It is only as a musician that Wagner will live, and to a musician the particular philosophy or philosophies that he preached in the *Ring* and *Tristan* and *Parsifal* are matters of very small concern. Wagner himself was always inclined to overestimate the importance of his own philosophizing, and his vehement garrulity has betrayed both partizans and opponents into taking him too seriously as a thinker.[7]

Newman's bluntness is refreshing, but once more he overstates his case. One does not make the pilgrimage to Bayreuth solely or even primarily to further one's awareness of the intricacies of political philosophy. Nor should the poem for the *Ring* be studied with this purpose in mind. One reads Hegel and Marx and many others for wisdom about the real world; one reads—or, more accurately, attends to—Wagner for the same purpose only if one is too philosophically naive to merit calling one's efforts philosophical.

Nevertheless, studying the *Ring* to discover philosophical truth about the world as it is (or as it should be) is quite different from studying the *Ring* to discover philosophical truth about the world as Wagner saw that truth. Whatever philosophy is embodied in the *Ring* remains inadequate to the complexities of the non-Wagnerian world—this claim may simply be asserted categorically, since the point is, as such, largely irrelevant to the purely critical purpose of this study. But understanding Wagner's philosophy is essential to appreciating and understanding the *Ring*. By philosophy here, I mean, in Nietzsche's fine phrase, a *Gedankensystem*, a system of thought without the conceptual forms of thought, but thought nonetheless. As I have already argued, whether or not the thought in this system is true independent of the *Ring* as a work of art need have no bearing on the integration of that thought within the overall aesthetic structure of the *Ring*. Newman apparently overlooks this point, as does anyone who rejects the *Ring* because its thought represents, or can readily be construed as representing, a world that differs sharply from the world most of us wish to preserve. The distinction between aesthetic truth and philosophical truth perhaps does a disservice to Wagner's own intentions, since he envisioned his work as being both philosophy that was great art and art that was philosophically true. But, perhaps with "The Ride of the Valkyries" resounding in our ears, let Thomas Mann make the crucial point in his own inimitable way: "We should be children and barbarians to suppose that the influence of art upon us is profounder or loftier by reason of the heaped-up volume of its assault upon our senses."[8] However, we should be just as "childish" not to approach the *Ring* as a complex structure of thought on a fairly high plane—but not so high that it can compete with philosophers who do their thinking with arguments rather than with images, stagecraft, and leitmotifs.

The poem of the *Ring* has now been detached from several related interpretive attitudes and stances which, I have argued, are in the present context either misconceived or misdirected. But any interpretation will have presuppositions, and it is, or perhaps should be, incumbent on the interpreter to be as forthright as possible in acknowledging these presuppositions. The more information brought into the open concerning the principles that underlie these presuppositions, the greater the latitude in determining the relative strengths and weaknesses of the interpretation that follows upon an adherence to these principles. The critical presuppositions employed in this study may be presented in both negative and positive settings. First, I state those principles which exclude sources of information that I do not believe to be especially relevant for present purposes.

1. No mention is made of the mythological source material Wagner worked into the *Ring*. After all, one can have the most minute knowledge of all the

original myths, legends, and sagas on which the *Ring* is based and still misunderstand the significance of the *Ring* itself. This possibility is real for the simple reason that the structure of the *Ring* is *different* from the literary sources which grounded that structure. Therefore, an interpretation of the *Ring* of the type that I shall offer should be based primarily on the text of the *Ring* as it stands, rather than on the various differences that exist between Wagner's retelling of the myths and the original myths themselves.

2. The second critical principle to be excluded here is a close corollary of the first. For if an interpretation of the *Ring* must follow the text of the *Ring* as it stands, then that interpretation should be based on the *final* text of the *Ring*, not on the various stages that marked Wagner's creation of that final text. By studying the historical sequence of the alterations Wagner introduced into the narrative, one may achieve a certain insight into reasons why the plot takes this turn of events rather than that turn, as developed in an earlier version. But the significance of a given event must ultimately rest on its place in the final version of the *Ring*, not on the comparative differences between any two versions with respect to this event.

Let me develop this point by commenting on another remark by Ernest Newman, who, to judge from this remark, would probably not agree with the contention I have just put forth. Newman writes: "Whether the course of Wagner's thinking in [the *Ring*] can ever be made entirely clear is open to doubt: the more one studies the drama the more conscious does one become that the process by which it was built up over so many years inevitably led to a certain confusion in Wagner's mind with regard to one or two elements in it."[9] Newman has raised an important problem in interpretation, but not for the reason that he thinks justifies it as problematic. There was, apparently, confusion in Wagner's mind about some elements in the *Ring*'s structure. But it hardly follows that the drama is "inevitably" flawed because the process of creating it did not proceed smoothly. The existing flaws in the *Ring* are flaws because they disrupt the organic unity of the *final* version of the work, not because discrepancies or inconsistencies emerge when comparisons are drawn between various intermediary versions and the final version. Thus, if Newman considers a discrepancy between one version of the *Ring* and the final version to be a flaw, he is surely mistaken. Such a flaw is only a discrepancy arising from different versions of the *Ring;* as such, it is a flaw only relative to the process of creating the final version and may well be completely irrelevant to the final version as a unified whole.

An example of a legitimate flaw would be an inconsistency in the final version as it stands—for example, when a character says one thing at one time and something different about the same thing in the same respect at a different time. Newman quite rightly indicates one such flaw in his *magnum opus* on Wagner.[10] But great care must be taken before other apparent divergencies are accepted as discrepancies that are also flaws in a damaging sense. All inconsistencies are discrepancies and are more or less harmful to the organic quality of the narrative structure for that reason. But discrepancies need not be inconsistencies. Characters in the *Ring* frequently refer to the same events in different ways at different times; as a result, the careless student may be tempted to construe these variations as discrepancies or even as inconsistencies. My policy has been to assume that variations are not discrepancies (much less inconsistencies) until there is no other recourse but to accept them as discrepancies. For if one hastily concludes that an apparent divergence is a manifest discrepancy, then one risks missing a subtlety in the narrative for the sake of eliciting a fault in the structure which may not be a fault at all, but merely further testimony to the intricacies of Wagner's genius.

3. Only cursory attention is given to what Wagner himself has written on the meaning of the *Ring*. First, and most important, because that aspect of the work which I shall develop is not considered in depth in Wagner's own critical writings. Second, because even if Wagner did treat the function of contracts in the *Ring* in detail, it would not necessarily follow that the content of that treatment would be helpful, much less incisive, much less definitive.

Wagner the critic interpreting Wagner the artist raises a number of problems in the theory of interpretation. For example, in answer to the question of why the gods must still perish after the gold has been returned to the Rhine, Newman cites the reply given in Wagner's famous letter to Roeckel: ". . . the necessity of the downfall springs from our innermost feelings, as it does from the innermost feelings of Wotan. It was thus important to justify *by feeling:* and this happens of itself when the feeling follows the total action, with all its simple, natural motives, in complete sympathy from beginning to end." Newman then remarks about the letter as a whole: "It is manifest enough from this confused statement that the reason why Wagner does not give a plain answer to Roeckel's plain question is that he cannot do so."[11] But Newman's judgment is premature. Wagner could perhaps have answered this question if: (*a*) he had been corresponding with someone with the kind of intelligence receptive to a properly abstract answer to such a penetrating question—on the assumption, perhaps unfounded, that Roeckel was not of such a sort; or (*b*) he himself had been in a better mood for such intellectual labor—Wagner may have been simply tired when he wrote the letter, or at least that part of it in question; or (*c*) he had been a better critic of his own work. There are numerous possibilities that must be explored before Newman can maintain the truth of his judgment. In fact, the only reason that adequately explains why Wagner could not answer this question is that the very structure of the *Ring* does not allow it to be answered. And, of course, if the *Ring* is so structured, then neither Wagner nor anyone else could answer the problem for the simple reason that it is unanswerable by the very nature of the problem that the question raises.

The creation of a work of art differs in principle from the re-creation of that work in the process of criticizing it. Some artists are good critics of the work of others, some artists are good at criticizing their own work and unconvincing when they deal with the work of others, and some artists are simply inept critics, regardless of whose work they examine. But even if one does assume that Wagner is a sound Wagnerian critic (both Nietzsche and Mann expressed doubts on this point), it hardly follows that Wagner's self-criticism exhausts the topic. The structure of the *Ring* is so complex that it is doubtful whether even its creator could, during or after the fact of creation, trace all the ramifications of that structure. [12] And it is even more dubious if Wagner's own multifaceted nature is taken into account, especially with respect to what he was or was not likely to think of his own work.

Until shown otherwise, the *Ring* should be taken as an organic unity with all its parts cohering with one another according to principles of aesthetic consistency. Given this unity, it is perhaps unavoidable that the social and moral implications drawn from that unity will conflict with some of Wagner's prose writings on social and moral matters. But such conflicts are rooted more in the peculiar vagaries of Wagner's character as a man than in dramatic or philosophical flaws proper to the *Ring* itself. The welter of Wagner's prose writings from 1848 to 1876 and, by reason of varying moods and shifting fortunes, the manifest and often contradictory changes of position on the issues addressed in these writings make any attempt to bolster an interpretation of the *Ring* by appealing to this body of work highly dubious. [13] However, on the assumption that our interest is in Wagner the thinker through poetry and music rather than in Wagner the thinker through prose, then the fact that the letter of the *Ring* is kept apart from the letter of Wagner's other writings need arouse no fear of distorting the sense of the work. The purpose of this study is not to measure the limits of consistency between Wagner's artistic poetry and his philosophical prose, but rather to focus on one aspect of one product of his art and to disclose the significance of that aspect within the work of art as an aesthetic whole.

4. In the same general vein, I shall not attempt amateur psychoanalysis by moving back and forth between events or characters in the *Ring* and apparently related events or characters in Wagner's personal life. The secondary Wagnerian literature contains many such attempts. I believe that studies of this sort are relevant in outlining the relation between the life of the artist and his work. But I also believe that such studies frequently concern that relation to the detriment of the work as such. This little book concerns the *Ring*, not the moods or predicaments Wagner was in when he wrote the *Ring*. Mixing biography, psychotherapy, and criticism—Newman, Robert

Donington, and Theodor Adorno (to a lesser extent) are all well-known cases in point—often leads to critical assertions about the work of art which are really claims based on merging the character of the artist and the product of his art. If the distinction between artist and art is not preserved, then the critic basing an interpretation on the reaction to the artist risks pronouncements about the work of art which are merely restatements of his personal attitude toward the human character behind that work. Wagner and his art are especially susceptible to such analysis in view of the inescapable fact that Wagner the man was such an inscrutable blend of the sacred and the profane.

The above account will suffice for those principles of interpretation based on the exclusion of certain types of information. The positive principles may be developed by introducing a distinction between interpretations based, respectively, on external and internal symbolic frameworks. A critic employing an *external* symbolic framework produces an interpretation based on a structure of images or concepts that are external to the images and concepts contained literally in the work under scrutiny. A critic employing an *internal* symbolic framework produces an interpretation based on a structure of images or concepts found within the literal content of the work. There are important differences between these two types of interpretation, and I shall now explore some of these differences.

Two well-known interpretations of the *Ring* that apply an external symbolic framework are Shaw's *The Perfect Wagnerite* and Robert Donington's *Wagner's "Ring" and Its Symbols*. Shaw examines the *Ring* in terms of the concepts of a type of socialism that differs from anything socialistic Wagner could have known about; Donington examines the *Ring* from the viewpoint of Jungian psychology. Neither interpretation contradicts or seriously conflicts with the other, since each interpretation is based on a symbolic framework which differs fundamentally from the other. Both interpretations are illuminating and important. It is further testimony to both the intellectual and aesthetic range of the *Ring* that, without suffering undue distortion, it can yield insights into such disparate interpretive frameworks as socialism and Jungian psychology. We may even be tempted to claim that the *Ring* will be impervious to distortion regardless of the specific content of the symbolic framework applied, however inapposite that framework may appear at first glance. Nevertheless, there are dangers in such procedure, and boundaries should be described, or at least noticed, so that these dangers are minimized.

To illustrate this point, consider how Donington deals with Wotan and his relation to contracts or bargains (as Donington calls them). Donington admits that contracts are the means whereby "Wotan has buttressed his power and established his worldly authority" (p. 135). He then describes the conflict that ensues as a result of these contracts: "On this level, Wotan's problem is that each such bargain, though safe-guarding some aspect of his authority, does so at the cost of concessions which limit that authority in another aspect, until eventually he has lost all liberty of action. He cannot break his bargains without destroying respect for authority in general, including his own authority" (p. 136). But this problem is, in an important sense, only superficial. Donington insists that, on a deeper and apparently more signifi- cant level, Wotan's situation "has to do not with outside bargains but with the unconscious inner bargains which from earliest infancy we begin to strike with ourselves and with our environment as we experience it" (p. 136). Donington concludes that in this sense, "Wotan's bargains are his inhibi- tions . . ." (p. 137).

Two levels are introduced in Donington's interpretation. The superficial level supports the external social and moral implications consequent upon Wotan's contracts, while the deeper and more important level is that defined by Wotan's internalized inhibitions. For Donington, the second and deeper level is the more decisive of the two, that is, the tensions in Wotan's personality insofar as these tensions are mirrored in the social strictures in his contractual relations with other characters. Donington's decided prefer- ence for one level rather than the other directs the course of his interpreta- tion, based as it obviously is on Jungian principles. What, for Donington, is tantamount to the superficial level of interpretation—Wotan's contracts in relation to the genesis of his power and authority—is an example of an internal symbolic framework. And Donington's reduction of this institutional aspect of contracts to the psychological aspect of inhibitions is an example of an external symbolic framework. But surely we would not overestimate the structure of the *Ring* by considering it sufficiently complex to accommodate *both* levels of interpretation, i.e., by discerning the significance of the institution of contracts from both a social and a psychological perspective. Donington's stress on the psychological at the expense of the social reduces the social level of interpretation to a mere extension of the psychological level. However, such a reduction effectively eliminates the social level from possible critical examination.

I believe that Donington's position illustrates the potential danger in emphasizing one aspect of an external symbolic framework at the expense of those symbols which are internal to the work. Let me state my point here with some care. I am not claiming that, in this case, an internal symbolic framework necessarily provides a better interpretation than an external symbolic framework—Wotan's emotions and personality are just as vital to the structure of the *Ring* as the social character of the contracts connected with these emotions and personality. But I suggest that it is a mistake to reduce one perfectly appropriate level of symbolism to another level of symbolism. And this is what Donington does when he implies that Wotan's contracts are, in reality, only a symbol of his inner inhibitions. A given image or concept or episode is symbolic in many ways and at many levels. There- fore, if Donington intends to maintain that the *Ring* is best understood as an exercise in Jungian psychology, he must give reasons to demonstrate his position. And, in the case of at least one of Wotan's contracts, it is difficult to see how he can maintain that position. How, for example, is Wotan's contract with the giants for the building of Valhalla an instance of an inhibition on the side of Wotan's personality? It appears to be a straightforward business transaction between a deity with the power to promise builders what they desire for their labors but without the power or the inclination to perform those labors himself. Why not then simply contract for what that deity wants? Donington's claim about the hidden connection between contracts and inhibitions, if generalized, implies that *any* business transaction, as long as it is contractual, is ultimately based on the inhibitions of the individuals who enter the contract. This conclusion may or may not be good Jung, but in the present context Donington is surely extending an application of Jungian principles beyond proper critical limits. At any rate, it is important to be alert to the dangers that arise when an interpretation based on an external symbolic framework is overextended.[14]

An internal symbolic framework is also susceptible to excess, but in a different direction. An interpretation based on internal symbolism approaches the work as a self-contained universe and then attempts to discern the important relation established between and among the various elements of that universe. To illustrate this type of interpretation and also one of the dangers to which it is prone, consider this claim by Kurt Overhoff in an incisive volume entitled *Wagners Nibelungen-Tetralogie:* "The ring of power forged by Alberich from the Rhinegold becomes the symbol of *fear:* all others tremble before the one who owns it. Its measureless anxiety is the magic through which they are dominated by the possessor of the ring."[15]

It goes without saying that the golden ring is one of the definitive elements in the cycle of music dramas named, in part, by that element. And the symbolic content attached to the ring as such will determine to a considerable extent the significance read into all the events that revolve around the production and pursuit of the ring. Overhoff identifies fear as the symbolic referent of the ring. One may presume that this identification does not imply that other elements of the *Ring* may not also represent fear, but it surely does imply that the ring itself is the predominant element symbolizing fear. However, one would do well to pause and ask whether the ring could not also symbolize something *other* than fear?

Two related problems arise at this point. First, to what extent is Overhoff's identification of the ring with fear legitimate? Second, if it is legitimate, does the identification preclude the ring from symbolizing something other than fear? As to the first problem, while it is generally true that those characters who know the capacity of the ring tend to view it with apprehension, does this fact justify identifying fear as the ring's sole symbolic significance? It would seem more appropriate to identify the ring symbolically with whatever *causes* the reaction of fear, not with the reaction of fear itself. Notice that Overhoff does mention the connection between the ring and power, but he then chooses to identify the symbolic function of the ring with the fear that the capacity and exercise of power tend to cause in those who lack the ring or are threatened by it. Which is more important—the power that the ring represents or the emotional reaction to that power? However this problem may be resolved, does it then follow that the predominant symbolic level *excludes* the less dominant symbolic level? My own conviction is that the ring would be more fittingly interpreted if it symbolized power rather than fear. But the point is that it can perfectly well symbolize both power and fear. Overhoff legitimately connects the ring with fear, but he then illegitimately overextends this connection to the point where the symbolic function of the ring as fear precludes the symbolic function of the ring from being anything other than fear.

This overextension can be traced to a misconstruing of a symbol as a one-level and static vehicle of significance. In noting one possible reason why Overhoff was prone to such a mistaken view, a danger peculiar to the mode of interpretation based on an internal symbolic framework may be articulated. After discerning the frequent conjunction of the ring with fear, Overhoff then generalizes this conjunction and isolates it as *the* symbolic function of the ring. But had he allowed the ring to interact with other elements in the *Ring*, he would not have so quickly identified the ring with (what I suggest is) one of its lesser symbolic functions and, more important, he would not have arbitrarily restricted the ring to only one of these functions. It is especially prudent when thinking through an interpretation of the *Ring* based on an internal symbolic framework to assume that the symbolic range of any element in the *Ring*—especially the golden ring itself—is as extensive as the universe of the *Ring* as a whole. The resulting interpretation will become more penetrating, the more each symbolic element is allowed to display its own function by interacting with as many other elements as the scope of the interpretation feasibly permits. The interpreter may still be guilty of over-looking something important or of overemphasizing something which is not important. But the knowledge that his method is subject to these dangers should help more than hinder the formulation and the development of a worthy interpretation, especially if the student of Wagner wishes to approach the high status of the "perfect Wagnerite."

The following interpretation is based on an internal symbolic framework revolving around the institution of contracts (*Verträge*). As noted in the Preface, the interpretation attempts to situate the importance of contracts and oaths within the world of the *Ring* and to comment on their relations to the various characters who become involved in this institution. I trust that the fact that this interpretation focuses on contracts and oaths will not leave the reader with the impression that the poem of the *Ring* is little more than a dry-as-dust exercise in legalisms. One might point out that any narrative that is replete with dwarves, dragons, lusty deities, talking birds, and magic potions can more appropriately be considered as a fairy tale than as anything else. But the dimension demarcated by the institution of contracts does in fact touch all these "playful" elements in the *Ring*'s structure, not to mention that this dimension is crucial to the understanding of its mortals and divinities and their basically human dealings with one another. It would, of course, distort the *Ring* to study it as merely an abstract legal tract, since the *Ring* is a fairy tale and much more than that besides. But it would also distort the *Ring* not to take into account the theme of contracts and oaths, especially since that theme has been so carefully integrated into the complex structure of the *Ring* as a whole. The sole purpose of the following study is to present a coherent and comprehensive account of that one theme. Once this account has been allowed to make its case, the reader will have what I hope is another useful perspective on the *Ring*, one which should aid both the thoughtful and emotional appreciation of a great work of art.

2

Contracts and Oaths in the Ring

Contracts and the Origin of Power

The final curtain has fallen on *Götterdämmerung*.[1] The Rhine has overflown its banks; Wotan and his regime have been annihilated by fire. But precisely why is the conclusion to the *Ring* so ultimate, so cataclysmic? Chapter 2 shows how an answer to this question may be secured by exploring the essential connection which joins Wotan and his divine regime to the non-divine world. Once we have an explanation for Wotan's fall from power, then the reason why a significant part of the world fell with him should become more evident.

At the beginning of *Das Rheingold*, Wotan rules the gods, the heavens, and all that is beneath the heavens. But Wotan did not always rule. In the long monologue from the second act of *Die Walküre*, Wotan reveals that his youth was spent in a ceaseless quest for love. But this passion was either replaced or sublimated by the desire for power, a desire which was satisfied when Wotan "won the world" (*gewann ich mir die Welt*). How did Wotan achieve this end? Wotan offers no explanation at this point in the *Ring*. He does, however, admit that during his past he practiced treachery and became "bound through contracts, which concealed evil" (*band durch Verträge, / was Unheil barg*). Presumably Wotan's acts of treachery occurred *after* he won the world. But, as we shall see, there is evidence to suggest that the very winning of the world was also an action marked by treachery, by a breach of nature in which lay a malignant evil. Once unleashed by Wotan's ambition, this evil would eventually consume both gods and heroic mortals before it had run its course.

How then did Wotan win the world? In the prologue to *Götterdämmerung*, the Norns provide the most substantial account of this epochal event. The first Norn recounts Wotan's early history and how he came to drink at the spring of wisdom (*Weisheit*), paying the eternal toll (*ewigen Zoll*) of an eye for the enlightenment he received. But wisdom alone is insufficient to win the world. Even the wisest ruler must have power as well. The first Norn goes on to describe how Wotan received this power from the world ash tree (*Weltesche*), from which he broke off a branch and fashioned a spear. The second Norn then reveals that Wotan carved records of contracts (*Verträge*) on this spear. As a result, the spear became the instrument of power and authority "he held as guardian of the world" (*hielt er als Haft der Welt*).

The process and principal implications of Wotan's transition from adolescent lover to adult ruler may now be described. The sequence of events as recorded by the Norns is important and should be preserved: first, Wotan receives wisdom as he drinks from the spring; then, power is bestowed on him after he breaks off the branch of the ash tree; finally, Wotan carves records of contracts on this branch as a tangible sign of his guardianship over the world. Nature is the source both of Wotan's wisdom (via the spring) and of Wotan's power (via the branch of the ash tree). Thus, nature must have possessed the capacity to transmogrify herself into these particular forms prior to the emergence of Wotan's desire to possess them. Furthermore, nature does not exhaust herself by bestowing the conditions of world rule on Wotan, since both before and after this event the waters of the Rhine continue to flow and the trees of the forests continue to blow in the wind. Nature must therefore have kept to herself stores of energy even more primordial than those which provided the wisdom and power granted to Wotan. A conclusion from this line of thought begins to take shape, a conclusion that at this point can be only provisional. The process that allowed nature and Wotan to interact and sanctioned Wotan's right of legitimacy is in some sense derivative and less primordial than the full source of that legitimacy. This process is, in fact, the institution of contracts.

Wotan's power depends on his right of authority. But Wotan's right of authority depends on exchanging an eye for the opportunity to partake of nature's wisdom. This decision, freely chosen, binds Wotan to nature in a distinctive and ultimate way. For in consenting to this exchange, Wotan also consents to the process through which such an exchange was possible. Stated abstractly, Wotan in effect enters into a contract in order to attain wisdom: If Wotan sacrifices one of his eyes to nature, then nature provides Wotan with wisdom. This wisdom then dictates that in order to win the world and to preserve what he has won, Wotan must also embrace not only the fact of this particular contract, but also the very institution of contracts as such. The originary exchange of an eye for wisdom is the natural foundation for the genesis and subsequent implementation of the institution of contracts. All other contractual exchanges, whether by Wotan himself or by anyone else (and regardless of the specific conditions of the exchange), are legitimized by this first fundamental contract between Wotan, the emergent ruling deity, and nature, the source of wisdom and power. Furthermore, since this institution is the means by which Wotan achieves and maintains the guardianship of the world, *all* subsequent actions—whether human or divine—performed in the name of wisdom and for the sake of legality receive their ultimate sanction from that wisdom which began to flow by virtue of Wotan's epochal interaction with nature. The universal scope of this ramification is of crucial importance for two reasons: first, because this epoch of world history dates from and is derived from Wotan's decision to guard the world on the basis of the institution of contracts; second, because this institution will not be restricted to purely legal contexts, but in fact will pervade the actions, attitudes, and emotions of all the inhabitants of that world.

Wotan achieves the administrative vision he will need to rule by decreasing the purely optical vision of his senses. Thus, Wotan is granted the capacity to wield the spear which is itself both powerful and also representative of power only *after* he has exchanged part of his natural optical vision for the vision required to exercise that power wisely. Furthermore, Wotan maintains his exalted station precisely in virtue of the power, now institutionalized and legalized, which the records of contracts carved on the spear tangibly represent. When Wotan as the Wanderer meets Alberich in the second act of *Siegfried*, Alberich is quick to point out that the record of Wotan's contract with the giants to build the castle of Valhalla remains engraved on the Wanderer's spear, long after that particular contract has been fulfilled by both parties. And the thunder which frequently accompanies Wotan's use of the spear, as in his confrontation with Mime in *Siegfried*, is both an aural symbol of Wotan's power and a reminder of the essential connection between nature and its capacity to bestow such power, given that certain fundamental conditions have been and continue to be fulfilled.

A peripheral matter must now be touched on. One must bear in mind that Wotan receives wisdom and power from nature—not from some other quasi-divine or autochthonic source. We know that at least one such source does exist, a self-conscious being from whom Wotan could conceivably have derived the wisdom and the power to become the guardian of the world. That being is the "father" (*Vater*) who has enjoined the Rhinemaidens to guard the gold. He is mentioned in the first scene of *Das Rheingold* and in the first scene of the third act of *Götterdämmerung*. Who is this mysterious figure? Whoever he is, he occupies a position of considerable authority, since the gold soon to be sought by Wotan and others is capable of making its owner the mightiest of mighty lords. Although Wotan's own powers of paternity are widespread and he is referred to as "father" in a number of (usually war-related) contexts,[2] there is reliable internal evidence to prove that this father could not have been Wotan himself. Thus, the condition laid upon ownership and exercise of the gold's power—that one must first renounce love—must have been known by this father, since he is the only possible source for the Rhinemaidens' knowledge of this condition. But if Wotan was the father mentioned by the Rhinemaidens, then Wotan must have known about this prerequisite *before* Loge informed him of it in the second scene of *Das Rheingold.* The mere fact that Wotan must question Loge about the gold must surely imply (on the assumption that Wotan is not deviously masking his knowledge) that Wotan did not know about the gold's latent powers. Furthermore, when Loge announces that the power of the gold can be released only on condition that the possessor of the gold foreswear love, Wagner's stage directions have Wotan turn away "displeased" (*unmutig*). These actions, both verbal and visual, seem sufficient to prove that whoever the mysterious *Vater* may be, he is not Wotan.[3]

The assumption here has been that this unknown father was the original guardian of the gold. But this assumption does not imply that he is also the source of the gold's power. The father must have some vestige of real power simply to be in a position to entrust the gold, rather unwisely as it turns out, to the protection of beings other than himself. But this power need hardly be equivalent to the power which flows from ownership and correct disposition of the gold itself. And, with this conclusion, further speculation on the nature of this shadowy figure becomes unnecessary. It is known that he is not Wotan, and there is no reason to think that his position is in any way essential to Wotan's acquisition of wisdom and power. Thus, as I have argued, Wotan assumed his high stature as world guardian only from his willful involvement with nature.

The records of contracts are indelibly inscribed on Wotan's spear. As such, they attest to the necessity of contracts *in* Wotan's rise to power and *for* the continued exercise of his authority. Wotan's partial blindness is his own personal record of this necessity. Although the graphic and primeval violence of nature may appear unnecessarily severe, there is good reason for such an exactment. True enough, succeeding instances of contractual exchange will rarely if ever be as self-destructive to the parties involved, but this, the original contract, must stand as the model for all other contractual relations. It is appropriate, therefore, that it involve the very summit of consciousness in the form of that being who will guard the affairs of the world and that it be drastic in quality so that all who will dwell in that world readily recognize its presence.

But even if the severity of nature's exactment from Wotan is granted as justified, one would do well to reflect further on the specific form which that exactment assumed. If Wotan's adoption of the institution of contracts is based on an encounter with nature, does it necessarily follow that this institution is itself natural in all respects? If nature as embodied in the form of Wotan is seriously and permanently injured by the loss of an eye, then could it be the case that nature as such is also seriously injured in engendering the process, the institution of contracts, through which Wotan suffered this injury? Is it possible that the demands placed on those who enter into contracts are somehow necessarily in conflict with their natural capabilities insofar as individuals can exist independently of the contractual institution? In one important sense, the answers to these questions are academic. Given the onset of culture in the form of institutionalized legal and social conventions, Wotan himself as well as all others who exist under his rule must act in accordance with those institutions as long as this particular form of culture continues to play out its history. But although in one sense academic, the problems raised by these questions remain pivotal. For, in fact, the history of Wotan's regime will terminate with the destruction of Valhalla. And since that regime had been established on the basis of the institution of contracts, the sense in which its demise is related to that institution must be determined.

Let us approach the problem by returning to the possibility, mentioned earlier, that Wotan's original contract with nature may have contained the seeds of his own destruction. According to the account of the Norns, Wotan's original contracts were "true" (treu). But according to Wotan's own testimony in Die Walküre, he was bound through contracts which "concealed evil." Do the true contracts attested to by the Norns overlap with the evil contracts confessed to by Wotan? It is evident that Wotan's contract with the giants in Das Rheingold was one in which evil was concealed, since Wotan had to become a thief in order to fulfill that contract. However, Wotan admits to evil "contracts," that is, more than one. Of course, Wotan could be referring simply to contracts similar to that perpetrated with the giants. But perhaps he was also referring to the fact, recognized by him only gradually and after considerable torment, that the foundational contract which empowered him to rule was itself inherently evil. Hidden in the very structure of that original contract was a force of evil which destined the demise of Wotan and his regime, an evil which began to manifest itself during the very process of legitimacy which allowed Wotan to assume power in the first place.

Under this interpretation, Wotan lost far more than the sight of one eye when he drank from the spring of nature's wisdom. For if he was free in his youthful search for love, he became bound to a destiny of doom in his adult quest for power and glory. The damage done to his optical vision spreads malignantly to his administrative vision, which will become clouded and corrupt, and also to the very institution of contracts allowing him to administrate, which will contribute to the corruption of all those who become involved in its constrictions. The unnatural condition of Wotan's partial blindness mirrors the universal unnaturalness of the institution which occasioned the acceptance of that partial blindness. The practice of making and keeping contracts then becomes an institution more artificial than natural, more conducive to breeding evil excess than wise administration. It is true, of course, that since Wotan freely chose to embrace this institution, the fault may lie simply in his own inability to exercise power wisely. But if the institution is in fact a breach of nature from which evil must flow, then Wotan was doomed from the very outset, regardless of the presence or absence of virtue in his own personal actions.

The dimensions of this difficult problem in interpretation extend to a number of issues with a rich philosophical heritage, of which the status of the state of nature and the relation between free will and determinism are only the most obvious.

For our purposes, the general scope of the problem may be defined by the statement and implications of a relatively abstract dichotomy. Either the institution of contracts is intrinsically natural or it is in some sense unnatural and artificial. Consequences of ultimate import will ensue, regardless of which alternative proves to be the case. If the institution of contracts is natural, then a violation of that institution will necessarily disrupt the even harmony of nature. Should the disruption reach certain proportions, then nature will resort to cataclysmic ends in order to purge the abuses directed toward itself, whether these abuses are of human or of divine origin. Furthermore on the basis of this interpretation, there is no reason to think that the institution of contracts will not survive this cataclysm, since contracts are, in themselves, just as natural as flowing springs and ash trees. The second alternative suggests a different resolution, but only after an identical conclusion to this particular epoch in world history. If the institution of contracts is not intrinsically natural, then a violation of that institution will not disrupt nature, just as a fallen tree will not significantly disturb the flow of a river. However, the sheer imposed presence of such an artificial device at the core of a culture of epochal duration must eventually result in conditions so self-destructive to life that only global purgation can rid the world of that device. At this point, the principal difference between the two interpretations becomes evident. Under the first interpretation, the institution of contracts may remain in force, even after the destruction of Valhalla; under the second interpretation, this institution must be replaced by a principle or device of power sufficient to sanction the affairs of the world to the same extent as that provided by the now defunct institution of contracts.

To summarize: If the institution of contracts is intrinsically natural, the sequence of events in the *Ring* should justify the fact that a regime grounded on that institution is finally purged; if the institution of contracts is not natural, the same sequence of events should present at least an indication of whatever principle or device will replace that institution after Wotan's regime has suffered a violent demise. The next two sections sketch the structure and ramifications of individual contracts and oaths as a type of contract, thus providing background to determine the status of the institution of contracts with respect to the dichotomy just outlined. In chapter 3, I shall conclude this study by arguing for that alternative which, in my opinion, most closely

approximates both the letter and the spirit of the function of contracts within
the symbolic universe of the *Ring* as a whole.

Contracts and the Preservation of Power

It has been shown that the source of Wotan's power is grounded in
contracts. And now I shall examine how the legitimacy of that power must be
preserved by contracts. Each of the following four subsections describes
contractual relations between Wotan and various individual characters or
types of character. The four subsections are arranged hierarchically, from the
base of the social ladder to its highest rung, i.e., from the giants to Erda.

Wotan and the Giants

Wotan's original need for the institution of contracts in order for him to be
in a position to "guard the world" is not made explicit until the prologue to
the final music drama of the *Ring*. But a specific contract occasions Wotan's
entrance into the dramatic action at the very outset of the *Ring*. When he
first appears in the second scene of *Das Rheingold*, the sleeping Wotan
dreams of power and fame greater than the power and fame he already
possesses. He awakes to discover that the tangible symbol of that power and
fame—the castle of Valhalla—is now ready for all the world to see. This
monumental edifice was constructed by the giants, who undertook the task
after settling on a contractual agreement with Wotan. The conditions of this
contract are straightforward. Wotan will receive the castle of Valhalla, the
product of the giants' labor, while the giants will receive the goddess Freia
from Wotan. But when the castle is completed and the giants arrive to
demand what has been pledged to them, Wotan refuses to release Freia and
orders the giants to substitute some other payment. The giants persist in
their demands, and Wotan becomes uneasy—for good reason. Freia is guardian of the golden apples, the source of the gods' eternal youth. If Wotan gives
the giants what they have explicitly contracted for, the gods will lose access to
her fruit and age quickly, perhaps even perish. But if Wotan does not give the
giants what they have contracted for, then Wotan defaults on the contract.
And when Wotan enters into a contract, the obligation to fulfill that contract
is no less binding on him than on the other party, regardless how "low" that
party may be in the world's social structure. How then is Wotan to extricate
himself from this dilemma, one of his own making?

The respective terms of this initial contract may be seen as a symbolic
evocation of the fundamental conflict that the institution of contracts imposes
on the principal characters of the *Ring*. The castle is grey, cold, lifeless. But
the castle is also solid, as solid in its own way as the present status of the

institution of contracts itself. At the opposite extreme, there is Freia, golden
in her youth and vibrancy, as full of that which makes life exhilarating as the
stony castle is devoid of life. And yet the two, one inanimate and the other
more than animate, are forcibly juxtaposed by means of a contract. The
tension between the solidity of what has been preserved from the past (the
castle) and the fluidity of what will be new in the future (Freia) appears to be
essential to the highest form of conscious life, for men desire to retain the
fruit of past labor at the same time that they yearn for the opportunity
afforded by the future. But, in this sense, Wotan, the guardian of the world,
must choose between these two equally desirable ends. And the conditions
circumscribing this choice are defined by a contract which Wotan himself has
engineered.

At this point, Loge appears, and Wotan presses him for wisdom to solve
the problem at hand. The crafty Loge disavows responsibility for the trou-
blesome contract, although it was upon his promise to redeem Freia somehow that Wotan agreed to the contract in the first place. Loge then reveals
the existence of the Rhinegold to the ensemble, telling of its power and
recent usurpation by Alberich. The giants' legitimate concern for Freia fades
as they envision what the gold could mean to them, so they seize Freia and
retain her as a hostage until the Rhinegold is theirs. They are perfectly
willing to exchange Freia for the gold, since the potential power of the gold
appears to be an equivalent or even greater good than Freia's charm and
youth. After Freia is borne away, the gods, including Wotan, begin to grow
pale and withered with age. Their very existence is threatened. Something
must be done. Wotan, with Loge as advisor, begins the descent into the
depths of the earth to win the gold and satisfy the giants' new demand. The
gods will then be preserved, and all will be right with the world.

The giants' reaction to Wotan's initial delaying tactics is significant. Fasolt
immediately berates Wotan for his apparent betrayal of the contract. He
reminds Wotan that "whatever you are, you are only through contracts" (*Was
du bist, / bist du nur durch Verträge*). Now the giants, by their own
admission, are ill-bred "clods" (*Wir Plumpen*). But although they may be
near or even at the base of the *Ring*'s social hierarchy, they are very much
aware of the origin of the power structure and its presence in the world in
which they must toil. Thus, when the golden treasure has finally been
handed over in payment, the giant Fasolt appeals to Wotan and to the gods in
general to divide the treasure "according to what is right" (*nach Recht*). The
precedent for such an appeal has been set far in the distant past. The giants
are aware of the precedent and in moments of stress they react instinctively,
even when Wotan has just acted against what is right by trying to renege on a
contract duly constituted.

By the product of their labors and by the magnitude of their bulk, the
giants represent a transition between the abstract character of a contract as

such and the very real effect contracts have on the existence of those for whom such devices are essential. The giants resemble, both in size and in demeanor, the castle which they have built. But the giants are alive while the castle is not, and although their level of awareness is not the most sensitive, they nonetheless know what is right and they also know that the substance of what is right depends on the institution of contracts. Thus, at the same time that Wotan is protected by the castle Valhalla, he is also threatened by the massive builders of that massive edifice, by their simple but true knowledge of why the wheel of civilized life continues to turn. The contract for the castle comes alive, as it were, in the imposing presence of the giants and their vocal recriminations toward Wotan in particular and toward the gods in general.

On his side, Wotan never contests their point about the fundamental relation between his position of authority and the fulfillment of contracts. In fact, during the second scene Wotan halts a potential altercation between Donner and the giants by extending his spear between them. Wotan exclaims "Nothing by force!" and adds that contracts (*Verträge*) are protected by the shaft of his spear. The intervention is effectively ironic, thus illustrating the compelling force of Wotan's authority and the reason for that authority. But this force applies to Wotan as well as to others. If the highest being can become obligated by contractual means to a level of consciousness at the low end of the social structure, then whatever has served to bind the extremes must also be capable of binding all intermediary levels. And a spear which enforces contracts made by non-divine individuals must, by virtue of consistency, also enforce a contract made by the divine wielder of that very spear. Such contractual bonds will be public as the bond between Wotan and the giants is public, regardless of whether they connect deities, giants, humans, or dwarves.

Wotan must make good his end of the contract while at the same time restoring Freia to the gods. For even if Wotan himself were exempt from the effects of her loss (which on Loge's testimony we know is not the case), a god who rules without his accompanying pantheon is not the god he once was, perhaps not a god at all. Whatever substitute will finally be found for Freia, the fact remains that the contract must somehow be honored. Wotan knows this fact, and he implicitly states the reason when he refers to Freia as "the sacred pledge" (*das hehre Pfand*). Fricka, Fasolt, and Fafner all refer to her in the same way, as a "pledge" (*Pfand*). It is essential to understand why Freia is, in Wotan's own words, "sacred" (*hehre*). She is sacred *because* she is a pledge and for no other reason, not even her crucial utilitarian role in the preservation of the gods' youth. Presumably any deity, or indeed anything at all, would be sacred, regardless of its intrinsic nature or instrumental value, as long as it is explicitly declared a contractual pledge. As pledged by the giants, the castle Valhalla is no less sacred in its stony silence than is the youthful vibrancy of the goddess Freia. Pledges are sacred because contracts are sacred, and contracts are sacred because they bind the primeval forces of nature to the conscious inhabitants dwelling in Wotan's world.

When, at the conclusion of *Das Rheingold*, the gold is finally stacked up in payment to the giants, Wotan feels "shame" (*Schmach*) deep in his breast. This shame is not merely the result of the profane spectacle before him with its affront to the nobility of Freia "the good" (*die Gute*). Rather, it is shame that follows upon the realization of his own actions in conceiving the contract that led to the present travesty. But such shame, however deeply felt, is only a prelude to the experiences Wotan will endure as a result of that ill-conceived contract. In fact, several emotions akin to shame also beset Wotan in this context, and they will be considered presently. But now, Wotan is caught in a problem of great urgency. The giants have heaped golden treasure in a pile shaped according to the outline of Freia's youthful form, just as they piled rocks according to the blueprint for Valhalla. And they have demanded that the golden ring cover the small slot in the treasure through which Freia's eye still shines. Until she is completely hidden by the treasure, the giants will not accept the gold as a substitute for the pledge Freia. The giants are sticklers for contractual details: if Valhalla has been constructed precisely according to architectural plan, then the treasure that stands as a contractual surrogate must also be delivered with commensurate precision. Needless to say, it is not accidental that only the ring, its power far exceeding its diminutive size and intrinsic value, remains as that one bit of gold which will satisfy the giants' sense of justice.

At first, Wotan is understandably adamant in his refusal to part with the ring. His passion culminates in the cry that he would not part with the ring "for all the world" (*um alle Welt*), although it is precisely for greater dominance of that world that he sought the ring in the first place. At this point, Erda appears, earth mother and source of natural wisdom. She emerges from a cleft in the rocks, thus suggesting by her entrance her close affinity with nature, with the substance from which Wotan has crafted a natural defense (Valhalla), and with the solidity of the institution of contracts. Her warning to Wotan to shun the ring, in concert with the pleas of the other rapidly aging gods, finally persuades Wotan to give up the ring. As all eyes converge on a deity deeply torn by both ambition and obligation, Wotan, the founder and guardian of all contracts, decides that he must fulfill this contract, not only to preserve the existence of his fellow deities, but also to preserve the institution which enabled him to become their ruler in the first place. The price Wotan is forced to pay is much higher than he ever anticipated, and the loss of the ring is a severe blow to his long-range aspirations. But greater still are the effects that would immediately ensue should Wotan *not* use the ring to redeem Freia and to preserve the sacred character of his original contractual pledge.

Just before he mounts the rainbow bridge to Valhalla, when apparently all is well with the gods, Wotan confesses that "care and fear" (*Sorg' und Furcht*) enchain his mind. Wotan has a presentiment of what lies ahead for himself and for the other gods. Even from the necessarily partial perspective of *Das Rheingold*, we may discern how Wotan has lost contact with the mode of behavior proper to a ruler who governs by means of contracts rightfully honored. This loss of contact takes two forms: (*a*) Wotan lacks the power, or at least the devious ingenuity, to fulfill the contracts he has made; and (*b*) more important, he does not have the wisdom to make wise contracts in the first place. A deity who has received and must preserve power through acceptance of the institution of contracts and their concomitant obligations must make wise contracts or else suffer the consequences that unwise contracts will eventually bring to his authority and to the power vested in him by virtue of that authority.

Wotan's confession of fear and care is an expression of an apparent paradox of emotions, since in general one is drawn toward the object of care and is repelled by the object of fear. As he approaches the rainbow bridge to Valhalla, surely Wotan should feel only confidence and optimism. However, fear and care replace this anticipated emotional reaction, thus extending and broadening the effect of Wotan's earlier sensation of shame. Wotan has been ashamed, partly because he intuited the real cause through which Freia, one of his own kind, was reduced to the status of a piece of merchandise in a business deal. Now, after the contract in which Freia was involved has been settled to the apparent satisfaction of all parties, Wotan's experience of fear and care serves as an emotional counterpart to the original tension noted above between Freia and the castle as emblematic of the status of contracts. Wotan cares for Freia and for all the gods, and he also cares for the whole system of order that he and the gods oversee; but Wotan fears that this system of order, and also the very existence of the gods, is threatened by a force that neither Valhalla nor any other divine artifice can withstand. As we shall see, the object of his fear will overpower the object of his care.

There is, I believe, important textual evidence to indicate that Wotan's failure to abide by the contract with the giants is an effect as well as a cause. The sense in which it is a cause is obvious: Wotan must become a thief, and an accursed thief as it will turn out, to fulfill the letter of the contract. But Wotan's failure in this instance is an effect if Wotan's position of authority has been gradually weakened as the result of other contracts on which he has defaulted. The evidence for this possibility lies in Wotan's offhand remark to Fricka that he never "seriously" (*ernstlich*) intended to hand Freia over to the giants. This admission implies that Wotan had made the contract with the explicit intention of not keeping it. To make a contract with the intention of keeping it unless dire circumstances intervene is one thing, but to make a contract with no intention whatsoever of keeping it is quite another matter. By his own admission, Wotan is in the latter position. Therefore, this type of dissimulation may not inappropriately be interpreted as a form of perjury, for although Wotan said one thing he did not mean what he said. In fact, Wotan is convicted of precisely this misdeed by Erda in the important first scene of the third act of *Siegfried*. Erda's reign as the source and purveyor of natural wisdom totters on the brink of cessation, but she retains sufficient stability to wonder aloud how Wotan, the "protector of oaths" (*Eide*), can rule through "perjury" (*Meineid*). The precise relation between contracts and oaths will be discussed shortly. The point here is that, although never guilty of perjury in the outright sense in which, for example, Siegfried perjures himself, Wotan is party to a contract that he never intended to keep. The statement that he would keep this contract was therefore a lie, and since the lie was uttered during a commercial enterprise legally sanctioned, that lie becomes tantamount to perjury.

The blithe and open manner in which he confesses his insincerity to Fricka deepens the impression that this was not the first time Wotan had violated that institution by means of which he became guardian of the world. Had Wotan never previously conducted himself in this manner, his initial default would surely have resulted in some considerable concern rather than in lighthearted mockery, especially since Wotan knew full well that contracts were the basis of his power and authority and could not for that reason be abused. Thus, in the second-act conversation with Brünnhilde in *Die Walküre*, Wotan expressly states that he is not allowed to "strike" (*treffen*) one with whom he has made a contract (*mit dem ich vertrug*). Presumably if force is disallowed, then so is deception, although future events will suggest that the latter is less liable to immediate reprisal than the former. Therefore, on the assumption that Wotan had been involved, with apparent impunity, in a series of contractual abuses, he would naturally be of the opinion that his present position was secure, regardless of what sort of liberties had been taken with past contracts. His careless attitude toward the contract with the giants thus epitomizes a long history of what will amount to a protracted exercise in self-destruction. On this particular occasion, however, Wotan's conduct has been such that he feels "care and fear." The prescient rightness of this reaction will be attested to shortly.

Wotan and Men

Wotan's contract with the giants implies that he was neither a despotic tyrant nor a benevolent dictator. If either of these possibilities were the case, Wotan could simply have coerced or cajoled the giants to do his bidding. Of course, the fact that circumstances impelled Wotan to effect a contract with the powerful but cloddish giants would, by itself, suggest nothing as to his need to contract with men. For even if there is a specific difference in rank between men and giants, men and giants are alike in that both are by nature subservient to Wotan. However, Wotan himself reveals the need to establish at least part of his intercourse with men by means of contracts.

In the second act of *Die Walküre*, immediately after his account of the circumstances surrounding Brünnhilde's birth, Wotan discloses that the heroes (*Helden*) whom Brünnhilde was empowered to designate for service in Wotan's defense were men (*Männer*) formerly subject to laws based on "tarnished contracts" (*trüber Verträge*). These men were bound in "blind obedience" (*zu blindem Gehorsam*) to the dictates of the gods. But although those so designated are primed for battle, the heroes will, in fact, perform only one function, and that hardly a task fit for warriors. As Waltraute tells Brünnhilde in the third act of *Götterdämmerung*, they fell the ash tree as timber to fuel the tangible destruction of Valhalla and they do so at the behest of Wotan's own "silent gesture" (*stummen Wink*).

Thus, it is man who completes that definitive act begun by the god Wotan when, in order to inaugurate this epoch in world history, he broke off a branch from the very same ash tree. Now, as the climax of the *Ring* approaches, Wotan has exhausted the power derived from that tree; and Wotan himself is so exhausted that he must command men, and warriors no less, to finalize the destruction of the tree that once, by way of Wotan, served as the instrument for establishing the principles of world order. Furthermore, Wotan orders the complete destruction of the *entire* tree, thus ending once and for all everything that the ash had represented. Presumably those men who felled the ash tree are destroyed in the conflagration that will consume Valhalla and Wotan. But the warrior men are only the mediating force; Wotan is the real agent behind the destruction of the tree. However, the fact that both Wotan and his mortal warriors are destroyed by the ash tree's fire illustrates how intimate was the bond that the institution of contracts had imposed on both deity and man up to the very moment of that deity's final gesture of despair.

Wotan's confession to Brünnhilde concerning the tarnished contracts with men is as important for what it leaves in silence as for what it says. Wotan does not maintain that all men were bound to the gods, but only those men suitable for heroic exploits in warfare. The possibility remains either that those men who were non-warriors were not bound by contracts or that they were bound by contracts that were not tarnished. But considering that the atmosphere of the *Ring* is predominantly martial, the fact that those men standing in the vanguard of human affairs were subjugated by contracts is clearly more significant than any other possible connection between contracts and those mortals who were peasants and priests. Wotan does not mention the details of the contracts, either for gods or for men. But such specification is unnecessary; by Wotan's own admission they were "tarnished." Thus, regardless of the specific conditions of these contracts, the most important class of men were being unjustly treated in a manner perhaps similar to the way in which the giants had been unjustly treated. We also learn that these contracts became ineffective on the death of the heroes bound by them. Again according to Wotan, it was Brünnhilde's task to "prod" (*stacheln*) them into readiness for the strife Wotan envisioned as imminent for himself and all other denizens of Valhalla. But if the tarnished contracts had bound men *after* death to the same extent that they bound men before death, there would have been no need for Brünnhilde or anyone else to prod them to do what they were legally required to do by contracts anyway.

The fact that Wotan's contracts with men were tarnished once again indicates his lack of concern for the institution that legitimized his regime. But even more fundamental than this lack of concern is Wotan's need to enter into contracts with men in the first place, regardless of his subsequent treatment of those contracts. Unlike the contract with the giants, which Wotan never seriously intended to keep, there is no indication that Wotan had any intention of reneging on his contracts with men, including the one with his carefully chosen warrior defenders. Thus, it was in Wotan's power to dupe the giants (or so he thought), but it was not in Wotan's power to dupe men. In fact, Wotan *needed* the services of men. Therefore, the full context of Wotan's contract with the warriors implies a double weakness; first, in that his status as a ruling divinity becomes tantamount to the level of consciousness of those mere mortals who become essential for his defense even as he stands regally in the midst of his own castle; second, in that Wotan could guarantee the fidelity of men only by means of an institutional device such as a contract, rather than by, say, his sheer magnificence as a ruling deity whose very presence would command obedience from warrior and peasant alike.

Wotan and Fricka

The giants explicitly and men implicitly have attested to the fact that Wotan is what he is only by virtue of contracts. But Wotan's own contracts are not the only contracts that must be executed according to the dictates of justice and rightness. Wotan must also guarantee that *all* contracts will be upheld, regardless of whether or not he himself is a party to the contract or has any personal stake involved. It becomes evident, as events proceed, that his failure to uphold one particular instance of one kind of contract results in the generation of circumstances that will eventually lead to the genesis of the hero who will publicly demonstrate the end of Wotan's regime.

This protective aspect of Wotan's relation to contracts is revealed in the interchange between Wotan and Fricka at the beginning of the second act of *Die Walküre*. Siegmund and Sieglinde have fled Hunding's hut and their illicit conduct has roused Hunding to plead to Fricka for vengeance. After promising satisfaction to Hunding, Fricka, the "guardian of wedlock," berates Wotan because he does not punish this violation of the "holy vow" (*heiligen Eid*) of matrimony. Although Hunding's plea is directed to Fricka, it is crucial to realize that the real power behind her position as guardian of wedlock resides in Wotan. Wotan must bear the final burden of punishing those who have sinned against marriage. Given Wagner's stark characterization of Fricka, she would doubtless be more than willing to bypass Wotan in order to punish the wayward lovers herself. She cannot do so, however, and must instead appeal to her consort, the king of the gods, for his consent in preserving the holiness of the marital vows by avenging this particular violation of those vows.

But in addition to the threat against the sanctity of marriage, the angry Fricka points to the potential dissolution of the "holy kinship" (*heilige Sippe*) binding the gods together by "ties" (*Bände*) that Wotan himself had forged. For Fricka, this dissolution looms as unavoidable if Wotan allows these flagrant sins against marriage to remain unpunished. Although the ties apparently bind all the gods to each other, the relation between god Wotan and goddess Fricka is especially crucial. Early in the second scene of *Das Rheingold*, when Wotan is defending himself against Fricka's taunts concerning the ill-conceived pledging of Freia to the giants, he begins one response by noting that he had staked one of his eyes in order to win Fricka as his bride. However, as noted earlier, the Norns will tell us in the prologue to *Götterdämmerung* that Wotan lost an eye as recompense for imbibing nature's wisdom. The Norns make no mention of a wife, nor of anything having to do with marriage. Since Wotan is not blind (at least not optically blind), the two reports must concern the same eye. Is this a discrepancy in the poem, or is Wagner presenting two different but compatible aspects of one episode? I believe the latter alternative to be correct, although the subtlety of the point demands that it be elucidated. Once the special relation between Wotan and Fricka is described more fully, the sense in which their marital contract is paradigmatic for the kinship of the gods becomes more apparent.

When Wotan drank from nature's spring, he learned that contracts were necessary in order to establish and maintain his position as world guardian. One of these contracts concerned the institutionalization of mating, required to introduce order into the potentially chaotic interaction of the sexes. This order took the form of contractual conditions similar to marriage as traditionally defined, for instance, the imposition of fidelity upon both spouses. This type of contract was equally incumbent on both mortals and divinities. In fact, as far as Wotan himself was concerned, the contract of marriage was as important as all other types of contract for which he sacrificed his eye. For if the marriage contract was derivative in importance with respect to these fundamental contracts, then presumably Wotan would have been free to embrace or ignore marriage. The fact that it was essential to lose an eye when

he married must imply that the marital contract was another of the fundamental contracts which grounded Wotan's authority and power. This sacrifice
of partial vision shows that Wotan was bound to Fricka as closely as he had
been bound to nature for the right to partake of wisdom from nature's spring.
Therefore, if Wotan wanted to accede to world guardianship, he could not
avoid accepting the marriage contract as necessarily binding him and all who
wished to have complete and legitimate association with the opposite sex.
Wotan lost an eye not because he chose Fricka as his bride, but because he
chose the institution of marriage as part of the institution of contracts. This
particular type of contract is, as are all contracts, essential to the structure of
natural wisdom. Furthermore, it is a type of contract which enlarges the
scope of that institution. Unlike the contract with the giants for the construction of something tangible, the marriage contract unites two individuals
for the sake of purely intangible goals (however these goals may have been
defined when the parties joined by marriage were both deities).

Although Wagner does not describe the marital relation with the word
Vertrag (contract), he does use the word *Eid* (oath), in such a way as to
indicate that contracts and oaths are the same in several essential respects.
The most explicit textual evidence for this important identity is found in
Brünnhilde's self-immolation monologue at the conclusion of *Götterdämmerung*. Brünnhilde, while describing the character of her lover and husband Siegfried, first mentions his good qualities and then lists his failings.
She begins the latter by noting that Siegfried betrayed "all oaths" and "all
contracts" (*alle Eide, / alle Verträge*). But an examination of the poem will
reveal that Siegfried never enters into a contract, at least one explicitly
named as such. Therefore, if Brünnhilde is not merely indulging in rhetoric
(and the apocalyptic context hardly supports this possibility), then the close
connection of contracts and oaths suggests that oaths, of which Siegfried
takes several, are in some respect identical to contracts.

For present purposes, the equivalency between contracts and oaths may
be summarized as follows: (*a*) contracts and oaths are both rooted in natural
wisdom; (*b*) contracts and oaths both necessarily involve the imposition of
obligations and sanctions in the process of fulfilling their respective ends,
whatever these ends may be. These common properties do not, of course,
preclude differences between the two. Thus, contracts tend to issue in
tangible products (the castle of Valhalla) while oaths tend to obligate the oath-
taker to act in a certain manner (to tell the truth, to be a faithful spouse, etc.).
Two individuals joined by the oath of matrimony do not build a marriage in
the same way that workers build a castle for which they have signed a
construction contract. Furthermore, an oath will frequently allow the one
who takes it to display publicly by an explicit linguistic act the fact and even
the extent of his feelings for something or somebody, rather than merely to
indicate a pragmatic interest in the acquisition of some commodity, such as a

castle. The differences between a contract and an oath are real, but the crucial properties common to both as institutionalized devices nonetheless remain. And, in fact, a gradual increase in the importance of the oath as a type of contract will be witnessed from this point to the conclusion of the *Ring*.

If oaths and contracts are in several respects basically identical, then an oath is no less important than a contract, and the violation of an oath will have the same repercussions as the violation of a contract. And if it should turn out that Wotan has violated his own marital oath, then it would be naive to expect him to be particularly conscientious in punishing another's violation of the same kind of oath. In fact, Wotan is a philanderer of the first rank. In the second scene of *Das Rheingold*, Fricka is wondering how to bind Wotan to her, since she is "concerned about my husband's fidelity" (*Um des Gatten Treue besorgt*). At this point, it is premature to infer that Wotan had actually been unfaithful; Fricka merely says that she is concerned, not that she knows for a fact of Wotan's infidelity. But by the second act of *Die Walküre*, the poem indicates that Fricka's suspicions have been confirmed. Fricka announces to Wotan with righteous wrath that "you have continuously deceived your faithful spouse" (*Die treue Gattin/trogest du stets*). Fricka has faithfully kept her marital oath; Wotan has not. Thus, it seems probable that "continuously" refers to acts of deception concurrent with if not prior to Wotan's contract with the giants. It is known, from Wotan's own testimony, that he has sired the nine Valkyries by Erda. And Fricka's diatribe intimates that there have been other adulterous interludes with less majestic female personages during Wotan's frequent wanderings about the world, with one such union engendering the twins Siegmund and Sieglinde. In short, Wotan has been something less than a paragon of marital virtue.

It seems clear that these misdeeds are not insignificant. In fact, if interpreted strictly in light of the fundamental character of the institution of contracts, Wotan's violation of the marital oath portends his careless attitude and underhanded actions toward the contract with the giants, ultimately suggesting a reason why Wotan's regime has lost its legitimacy. A key factor in substantiating this interpretation is Fricka's mention of a divine kinship essential to the gods' existence. Although the bond which links Wotan to Fricka is necessarily unique, it is analogous to the bonds which tie all the gods to one another. If Wotan fails to preserve any one of these bonds, then the sacred kinship of the gods is threatened in its entirety. Even a divine chain is only as strong as its weakest link. Fricka forcefully indicates the potential threat to the gods in the second act of *Die Walküre*. At the conclusion of her harangue directed at Wotan, she impresses on him the need to protect her honor and her rights as protector of the sacred institution of marriage. If this right is not protected, Fricka warns that "we gods will be ruined" (*gingen wir Götter zu Grund*): hence Fricka's justified anger when

Wotan fails to react to the violation of an oath with the same stern justice that should be directed at the violation of a contract. It misrepresents Fricka's character to reduce her to a mere spokesman of conventional morality for conventional morality's sake. Fricka is not motivated simply by her injured pride and tarnished image, nor by slavish adherence to the morality of the day. She sees what Wotan apparently does not, that the illicit union of Siegmund and Sieglinde is unnatural, not only because it is adulterous and incestuous, but, more fundamentally, because it goes against the very nature of the contractual dimension essential to Wotan's position of authority and to all the gods insofar as they depend on Wotan for their own right to existence.

Fricka's concern for the contractual aspect of marriage and the implications of this aspect for the continued existence of the gods assume a certain air of poignancy once the probable history of her relation to Wotan is placed in view. It is known that Wotan as a young god was driven by a passionate desire for love. And it may be presumed that this desire was not completely quelled when, at a more mature age, he embraced the young Fricka as his bride. Now, however, neither appears to feel much in the way of desire for the other; the relationship has settled into an uneasy equilibrium, a sort of stale truce between one-time lovers. Fricka may seem to behave like the archetypal shriveled fishwife, but of course Wotan has not dealt fairly with her. Therefore, it is no wonder that her original love for Wotan, which may have equaled or even surpassed in intensity his original love for her, has at this point been rendered all but invisible by Wotan's almost systematic abuse of the contract that originally sanctioned that love. Are Fricka's admonitions to Wotan based purely on the natural instinct for her own self-preservation as a deity or are they also tinged with the love she once felt for the king of the gods? The possibility that the latter condition is still present in Fricka's shrill cries elevates her emotional state from straightforward anger to a more rarified mixture of resentment in conjunction with bittersweet memories of a kind of passion that will no longer be hers to share.

Wotan will avenge the wrong done to Fricka and to the institution Fricka represents. In fact, he swears an oath to her that he will do so (*Nimm den Eid!*). But when Wotan's spear does eventually avenge Fricka's shame at the end of the second act of *Die Walküre*, the damage to Wotan in particular and to the divine kinship of the gods in general has already been done. Wotan still controls the ultimate fate of Siegmund, but the fact remains that his hesitation allowed the union of Siegmund and Sieglinde to be consummated. Siegfried is the result of that union, and this mortal hero will break the same spear by means of which Wotan belatedly terminated the unnatural and illicit union which allowed Siegfried to be born. Had Wotan acted promptly in the discharge of his duty and seen to it that the sanctity of the marriage oath was preserved, had he recognized that an incestuous and adulterous union between lovers was not justified simply in virtue of their being lovers,

Siegfried would never have been conceived. Wotan may well have suffered the same fate as he in fact will suffer, but he would not have suffered that fate at the hands of a Siegfried unborn.

Nevertheless, it is difficult not to feel some measure of sympathy for Wotan, especially in view of the circumstances that, in part, define his predicament. Wotan must have felt erotic love for the woman by whom he sired the twins Siegmund and Sieglinde, and he must have sensed at least a tinge of paternal love for the twin children as they grew, became separated from one another, and then matured. When Wotan appeals to love in order to justify his offspring's adulterous and incestuous reunion before an affronted Fricka, he is therefore personally cognizant of the experience of love at several levels. Wotan's respect for the power of love, regardless of, in this case, its "unnatural" setting, is doubtless sincere, and it seems that only the coldest heart would reject the cogency of his claim. But the claim is, in fact, rejected. And the fact of this rejection is important, for it suggests that regardless of its origin and apparently self-justifying intensity, even the most passionate love cannot stand as a standard sufficiently powerful to sanction a kind of conduct which violates the letter of the existing standard of conduct set by contractual agreement.

Fricka's outrage at the union of Siegmund and Sieglinde seems to imply that this union was in all respects illicit, unnatural, and thus in no sense justified. But it is important to note that the relation between these two lovers is not based simply on some elemental form of congenitally shared desire. Shortly before the famous "*Winterstürme*" aria in the first act of *Die Walküre*, Siegmund vows that "the oath" which weds him to Sieglinde burns "in honor" in his breast (*brennt mir den Eid, / der mich dir Edlen vermält*). And just before he meets Brünnhilde in the second act, Siegmund refers to Sieglinde as his "sweetest wife" (*süssestes Weib*). There is good reason to think that Siegmund is not merely speaking metaphorically or wishfully. Regardless of how unnatural the union (or, in a sense, the reunion) of Siegmund and Sieglinde may be, Wagner still finds it expedient to sanction their union with an oath (*Eid*). But why?

The answer to this question may be derived from the fact that this oath, as all oaths in the *Ring*, entails a pledge involving both parties. At the conclusion of the second act, Siegmund threatens to kill Sieglinde and himself rather than face Valhalla without his sister-bride. However, Brünnhilde exhorts him to entrust his wife to her "for the sake of the pledge" (*um des Pfandes willen*) that he blissfully bestowed on Sieglinde. This pledge is the hero Siegfried, conceived during their night of love. The "pain and suffering" (*Schmerz und Leid*) Sieglinde will endure in giving birth to Siegfried—the extent of which suffering being duly noted by Brünnhilde in anticipation and by Mime in retrospect—complements Siegmund's intention to take his own life for the sake of love (although, because of Brünnhilde's favorable intervention on his behalf, he is not required to go to this extreme). In a sense, both Siegmund and Sieglinde attest to the tangible pledge of the marital oath by pledging their lives, Siegmund now for the love and protection of his bride in the face of the threat posed by the revenge-minded Hunding, Sieglinde later for dispassionate love of the tangible pledge instigated by her passionate love for Siegmund.

But is it necessary or merely fortuitous that the union of Siegmund and Sieglinde be sanctioned by an oath? My contention is that the logic of the *Ring*'s thought structure *requires* that this union be sanctioned by an oath. It should be noted that if the oath joining Siegmund and Sieglinde is basically an instance of the same kind of oath protected by Fricka's divine aegis, her wrath will be occasioned not only by adultery and incest, but by bigamy as well, at least on Sieglinde's part. Given this blatantly overt and triply immoral union, one would perhaps have expected Wagner not to sanction it with an oath. The union would then become the setting for a climactic confrontation between self-redeeming love and conventional morality, with the former triumphing over the latter by reason of the lack of restrictive tensions proper to contracts and oaths. But Wagner has not thought through the relationship between the lovers in this way. And the reason he has not is precisely this confluence of nature, unnatural excess, and love.

The need to sanction this union institutionally is based on the function to be performed by the unique issue of this union. That issue is Siegfried, the hero who will demonstrate by his actions the termination of Wotan's world rule. Recall that Wotan in his guise as a Walsung had fathered the twins Siegmund and Sieglinde by a mortal mother. Therefore, Wotan's own seed (once removed) will become the instrument by which he will manifestly cease to rule. Wotan rules in virtue of contracts, one of which is the marital oath. Thus, the fact that Siegfried's birth is sanctioned by the marital oath makes the generation of the mortal instrument of Wotan's destruction completely consistent with the principal condition through which Wotan ruled in the first place. For if Siegfried had been engendered *without* the sanction of the marital oath and had then performed the same heroic and world-consummating deeds, Wotan would have been destroyed by the mortal issue of a fundamentally non-natural bond, i.e., the unsanctioned union of Siegmund and Sieglinde. Had this union not been a properly sanctioned marriage, then whatever issued from its consummation would no longer fall under those events over which Wotan has authority and responsibility. His demise at the hands of Siegfried would then have been external insofar as it depended on the fateful coincidence of desire and intentions fulfilled outside of the contractual domain. But to allow destruction from an external source would not have consigned Wotan to a termination that included both his own person and the regime that he ruled. And this kind of universal disintegration is precisely what the narrative of the *Ring* will demand. Therefore, the marital oath between Siegmund and Sieglinde must be preserved in the same way that an oath must be preserved in all other contractual involvements that project the same or similar ends as the institution of marriage. The preservation of the conventional marital oath is a vital link in the sequence of contractual events Wagner has constructed with considerable dramatic and thoughtful subtlety.

The passionate love story of Siegmund and Sieglinde, in concert with its especially evocative music, contributes in large measure toward the popularity of *Die Walküre*, the most frequently performed single music drama of the *Ring*. The genesis and eventual fulfillment of the relationship between these two lovers is perhaps the most tender episode in the *Ring*, a work defined on the whole by most of the baser examples of human behavior. If one is appalled by the range and severity of the latter, then one is also drawn to the depth and sincerity of the former, for the love between Siegmund and Sieglinde shines brightly, although briefly, in a very dark world. This relationship focuses one's more elevated sensibilities on the presence of such love, both as it is actually played out in *Die Walküre* and, as a sort of counterpoint, in the final two dramas of the *Ring*. But the depth of emotional attachment to this episode should not be completely detached from the dimension of contracts and oaths that has touched even the pure intensity of this love. The contractual dimension, although apparently distinct from the immediacy of one's natural attraction toward the lovers, is no less real for not being at the center stage of the emotional involvement with the dramatic action before one. The love between Siegmund and Sieglinde is in stark contrast to the lack of love between Wotan and Fricka. But these two relationships, polar opposites with respect to the presence and intensity of love, are nonetheless identical in terms of their inclusion under the sanctioning authority of oaths in particular and the institution of contracts in general. One must therefore keep alert to the presence of an element crucial to the *Ring*'s structure, an element that would perhaps not receive the attention it deserves, given the passionate quality of the events of which that element is a part.

Wotan and Erda

Erda appears in two of the four music dramas, *Das Rheingold* and *Siegfried*. In the two music dramas in which she does not appear, she is referred to by other characters. When she first emerges, in the final scene of *Das Rheingold*, Wotan does not recognize her, nor does he seem to know who she is and how she belongs to the general scheme of things. But her warning that Wotan shun the ring with its attendant curse and her prophecy concerning the impending doom of the gods ignites Wotan's interest to know Erda more intimately. As Wagner's stage directions indicate, both Froh and

Fricka must step in to hold Wotan back from following her at that very moment. But Erda claims that there is no real need for Wotan to follow her in search of knowledge. Her last words before sinking into the earth from which she came include an admonition to Wotan that "you know enough" (*du weisst genug*). What does Wotan know? He knows that he has made an unwise contract, that he reneged on that contract, and that he became a thief in order to salvage what remained of that contract. Furthermore, Wotan knows all along that he was granted the right to rule on condition that the institution that served as the source of his legitimacy be protected by his guardianship. But *Wotan himself* has sinned against that institution and therefore against the primordial power of nature itself. By rights, and without having any recourse to Erda's vocal wisdom, he should "know enough" to recognize why he must suffer both the personal humiliation of "care and fear" and the much more extensive and final repercussions that such actions warrant. Nonetheless, sometime between the dramatic action of *Das Rheingold* and the dramatic action of *Die Walküre*, Wotan descends into the bowels of the earth in order to visit Erda and to learn from her what he feels he must learn, regardless of whether the knowledge is favorable or unfavorable to his own future.

Erda is primevally wise (*urweltsweise*); she knows "how everything was, is, and will be" (*wie alles war, weiss ich: / wie alles wird, / wie alles sein wird*). But Erda is also female, and although her wisdom is vastly more extensive than Wotan's, her powers of self-control are apparently such that she is either unwilling or unable to fend off Wotan's advances. In his long monologue in the second act of *Die Walküre*, Wotan reveals that he conquered her "with the magic of love" (*mit Liebeszauber*) and that she then granted him the desired "information" (*Kunde*).

The relation between Wotan and Erda during their involvement with one another must be described as precisely as possible. Wotan claims that he "conquered" (*zwang*) Erda by the magic of love and that in the process she broke her silence, began to offer "discourse" (*Rede*), and then provided him with the information he desired. The implication is, or appears to be, that Erda supplied the knowledge Wotan wanted solely in virtue of the coercive power of love's magic. But both the form and the content of the German text suggest that another dimension is present in addition to love. The poem reads:

> Kunde empfing ich von ihr;
> von mir doch barg sie ein Pfand:
>
> (I received information from her;
> but she secured a pledge from me:)

This text is constructed to suggest that an exchange of sorts took place between Erda and Wotan (*von ihr . . . von mir*). The "pledge" (*Pfand*), Wotan proceeds to reveal, is Brünnhilde and the other Valkyries issuing from their union, just as Siegfried was referred to as the pledge (*Pfand*) of the union between Siegmund and Sieglinde. Thus, although there is no evident reason to think that Wotan and Erda exchanged anything like a marital oath, at some point the two probably became involved, at least implicitly, in a quasi-contractual arrangement.

If, however, Wotan received knowledge from Erda, what did Erda receive in return from Wotan? The answer, I suggest, is the privilege granted to Erda of bearing a maiden who will marshall her eight sisters to do Wotan's bidding, i.e., to gather heroes in order to protect Wotan against the threat to his regime revealed by Erda herself. In reproducing beings whose function is to act in the world rather than merely to know about the world, Erda is effectively transformed from an essentially passive medium, the source of natural wisdom, into a source of weapons suitable for Wotan's defense. The details of this interpretation need not be pursued beyond the subtle significance hinted at by the presence of the term *Pfand*. Nevertheless, let us drive the general point home by situating the need for some interpretation of this form. Given the structure of the *Ring* as a whole, if Wotan has been involved in contractual relations with nature, gods, men, and giants, then we would expect the cycle to include his involvement with all levels of the *Ring*'s cosmological hierarchy. And here we discover just such a relation with Erda, a being distinct in kind from all other differentiated types in that cosmology. Thus, from the perspective of the contractual dimension, that relation is conspicuous precisely by reason of its tenuousness.

Erda, as the etymology of her name suggests, is the mouthpiece of earthly or natural wisdom; as such, she merely vocalizes what nature has already wrought in the spring of wisdom and by the ash tree of power. It is evident that Wotan's youthful fire for natural wisdom remained intense, at least up to and including his series of erotic unions with Erda. In fact, these unions reaffirmed his intimacy with nature, for Erda serves Wotan in a most tangibly natural manner by providing him with the Valkyries as visible defenders of the castle Valhalla. Thus, nature as personified by Erda also bestowed the instruments of defense for a regime that was founded on natural wisdom as emanating from a flowing spring. Even now, when this regime is all but moribund, Wotan actively pursues the most vibrant form of nature still extant, the somnolent Erda. His interest is based on a fusion of passion and calculative self-interest, the passion of his past relationship with Erda and the natural interest in self-preservation. But Erda, nature at its anthropomorphic apex, is no longer wise. All Erda wants to do is sleep. Wotan's desperate actions in the face of such dying greatness indicate the extent to which he is still linked to nature, especially nature in its most complex form and, what is particularly important, regardless of the state of that form. Even more telling is Erda's failure to respond, since this failure pregnantly evokes the extent to which nature has become devoid of the power required to sustain what had at one time been its most potent and resplendent form of expression, the emergence and growth of a world order under Wotan's guardianship.

Summary

The narration of the full extent of Wotan's involvement with contracts is completed during the second act of *Die Walküre*. Before the *Ring* is half over, we see how inextricably Wotan is caught in what might be termed a cosmological web of contracts and oaths. Wagner has skillfully integrated this abstract social dimension into the dramatic structure of the *Ring*. Thus, when Wotan first appears in both *Das Rheingold* and *Die Walküre*, he is immediately beset by confrontations based on the two different types of contractual exchange. In *Das Rheingold*, it is the contract with the giants for tangible property and the problem of fulfilling that contract without losing the source of the gods' youth. In *Die Walküre*, it is the contractual oath of marriage and the problem of punishing a violation of that oath as a necessary condition for preserving the gods' divine kinship. Wotan is directly involved in the contract; he is indirectly but still essentially involved in the oath. In both cases, however, Wotan's actions or lack of action have an immediate bearing on the welfare of all the gods. Furthermore, it is now known that Wotan had to contract with men in order to surround himself in time of duress with the protection of warriors. And the knowledge received from Erda was also won by the contractual device of a pledge, analogous in this respect to other contracts in the *Ring*. And finally, the very stuff of nature is closely connected to the institution of contracts: water, the source of the wisdom by which Wotan embraced that institution; wood, the source of the spear on which Wotan recorded contracts and by which he protected them; stone, the substance chosen by Wotan to provide some measure of defense when the regime founded on that institution is threatened; and gold, the precious metal, the source of power sufficient to topple the existing world order, regardless of its institutional foundation. As long as the staging of the *Ring* assumes some form of realism, it is perfectly possible for an attentive audience to sense the connections between visible nature in several of its forms and the invisible presence of the institution of contracts. The consistency that marks the visual and the linguistic elements in this particular dimension of the *Ring* should not go unnoticed, nor should the same consistency concerning the comprehensive integration of contracts and oaths within the full narrative of the *Ring*.

Wotan is therefore at the contractual hub of a turning wheel circumscribed by the cosmology of the *Ring*—nature, giants, men, gods, and Erda. His power as ruler is preserved precisely by virtue of his ability to maintain the harmonious interplay of this contractual wheel. Even the spectrum of his emotions as a deity of anthropomorphic form can be arranged according to his reactions to various contracts: anxiety, at his precarious involvement with the giants over payment for Valhalla; hope, at the prospect of securing an adequate defense for his regime from mortal heroes who had once been the subject of contracts; and joy, at the sight of love between mortals that is so intense that it appears to circumvent all existing contractual standards of propriety. Nevertheless, Wotan remains inscribed within the contractual wheel that he himself created. But where and how is this turning wheel destined to come to rest?

Contracts and the Loss of Power

There is an obvious sense in which the boundaries imposed above have been overstepped. In the course of laying out the universal extent of Wotan's contractual involvement, it became necessary to mention the lack of wisdom and outright illicitness of Wotan's actions when he deals with individual contracts. The implicit repercussions of Wotan's misconduct will find their explicit enunciation in the episodes considered below. These episodes approximate the narrative flow of the dramatic action. The first three parts focus on Wotan, the last three on Siegfried and Brünnhilde. The section as a whole depicts the inexorable progression of events leading to the ultimate destruction of Wotan and Valhalla as this progression is defined by Wotan's own contractual relations and by other characters, principally Siegfried and Brünnhilde, insofar as they participate in contracts and oaths of their own.

Wotan and Alberich

I have sketched above the relation between Wotan and contracts on all levels of the *Ring*'s social hierarchy except one, the level inhabited by the dwarves. Wotan does not contract with any of the dwarves in the way he does with, say, the giants, but he is directly involved in a contractual arrangement made by the dwarf Alberich. Although the crucial episode between Wotan and Alberich occurs after Wotan attempted to renege on his contract with the giants, the global implications of that involvement are such that the incident comprises the opening movement in Wotan's loss of power and in the destruction of the world order which he superintends. We therefore return to the opening scene of the *Ring*.

In the first scene of *Das Rheingold*, Alberich is frustrated in his pursuit of the comely but frivolous Rhinemaidens. They are frivolous because, while baiting him, they disclose for no apparent reason both the power of the gold shining in the depths of the Rhine and the condition that must be met before that gold can discharge its power. Alberich learns that only one who foreswears love can command the power now latent in the gold. For Alberich, reaching a decision in this matter is not difficult. He is runty and ugly in appearance, and love does not come readily to such individuals. Alberich does not hesitate to exchange love for an opportunity to wield power and to exercise world domination. He rips the gold from its natural resting place and then vanishes into the gloomy reaches of the Rhine. The Rhinemaidens cry out in soulful anguish, for the gold has been raped and the harmony of nature has been disrupted. The apocalyptic drama begins.

The Rhinemaidens are the first living beings to appear in the *Ring*. Their character is defined by skittish playfulness and, in particular, by the fickleness of their affections and attitude toward love. In a sense, their behavior may be seen to resemble the fluidity of the water that provides them with life. Although the initial confrontation in the *Ring* is based on love, that confrontation can only be comic in tone, given the inapposite nature of the partners in this type of prospective relationship. For at this point, the Rhinemaidens are no less distant from the standard of womanly excellence (exhibited later by other characters) than is Alberich distant from the equivalent form of male excellence. And yet this rather bizarre quartet cavorts in the waves, sporting with love. For the Rhinemaidens, it is an amusing diversion; for Alberich, it is a way to relieve the pressures of lust. Introduced in these surroundings, the love theme begins in a context of low relief. It is true, of course, that love in several forms will assume the highest importance later in the *Ring*. Nevertheless, the fact that the initial pursuit of love preoccupies creatures who seem incapable of love reveals something about love within the overall fabric of the world in which this confrontation occurs. For if, in this world, love can be so debased, to what extent will it be possible for love to be exalted?

The moral intricacies of Alberich's action here at the very outset of the *Ring* become evident only after that action has been distinguished into two different aspects. The mysterious father (*Vater*) has enjoined the Rhinemaidens to protect the gold so that, in their words, no "false aspirant" (*Falscher*) should carry it off. But the Rhinemaidens do not say that no one under any circumstances should claim the gold, only that no one who is inappropriate or false should be allowed to possess it. Once Alberich takes the gold, it is clear to the Rhinemaidens that he is a member of precisely this class, hence their cries of "robber" (*Räuber*), cries echoed by Loge and Wotan in later references to Alberich's deed. But Alberich cannot claim the latent power of the gold simply by *stealing* it from the Rhine. Only if Alberich also *foreswears love* will the gold yield the magic charms permitting the one who swears this renunciation to forge the gold into a ring. As a natural entity, the gold is little more than an object of beauty; as an artificial ring engendered by fulfilling the conditions reported by the Rhinemaidens, the gold becomes capable of providing power of cosmic dimension.

Therefore, although the actions of (a) stealing the gold and (b) foreswearing love for power are virtually simultaneous, they are also clearly distinct. Alberich himself points to the distinction just before he departs from the Rhinemaidens:

> entreisse dem Riff das Gold,
> schmiede den rächenden Ring;
>
> (I rip the gold away from the crag,
> and will forge the avenging ring.)

And he repeats this distinction during his confrontation with Mime in the second act of *Siegfried*.[4] One could conceivably steal the gold and rest content with it as a shiny treasure without also deciding to subject oneself to the condition required for unleashing its more extensive and potent properties. But Alberich has made precisely this decision, a decision with eventual repercussions reaching far beyond the fate of a frustrated dwarf.

The ramifications of both aspects of Alberich's deed are crucial, especially with respect to a morality that has its ground in nature. Stealing the gold is immoral. But it does not follow that foreswearing love for the possibility of exercising power is also immoral. The immorality of the first aspect of Alberich's deed does not necessarily imply the immorality of the second aspect of that deed. Exchanging love for power is perhaps a questionable choice as far as the dictates of natural wisdom are concerned, but this exchange is not immoral simply because it may be unwise. If Alberich steals the gold, then he has no legitimate right to possess the gold. But, given the fact of his possession of the gold, does it follow that Alberich also forfeits the right to exercise power once he sacrifices his capacity for love in order to attain that end? Wagner's poem suggests an answer. Since Alberich subsequently does exercise power (i.e., over Mime and his fellow dwarves in Nibelheim), the provisional answer to this question must be negative. And an important conclusion gained by distinguishing Alberich's deed into these two aspects may now be secured. The fact that Alberich falsely stole the gold is independent of the process of events set in motion after he foreswears love for power. And it is the latter process which turns out to be decisive as far as the outcome of the *Ring* is concerned.

When Wotan learns of the power controlled by the gold, he immediately desires to possess that power. Loge, never fastidious as far as moral niceties are concerned, candidly advises Wotan how he should proceed: "What a thief steals, that you steal from the thief." Wotan acts on this advice; he and Loge descend into the earth to appropriate the gold. Alberich meets them, is wary at first, but then succumbs to Loge's inducements to display publicly the potency of the Tarnhelm, a magical helmet of disguises constructed by virtue of the magic of the golden ring. When he foolishly transforms himself into a toad, he is immediately captured by the wily gods. And the price of release-ment is all too high: he must relinquish all that the gold has brought him. Wotan collects the Tarnhelm along with the treasure forged by the other smithy dwarves and completes his ravishment by seizing the ring, the vehicle of the Rhinegold's ultimate power. The deed is accomplished, as Loge reports later to the gods, by "cunning and force" (*List und Gewalt*). Justice and rectitude have played no role in the divine acquisition of the gold and its attendant powers.

Alberich's anger is extreme. If Wotan steals the ring, Alberich charges that this act will condemn the immortal Wotan to sin against everything "which was, is, and will be" (*was war, / ist und wird*). But what is the precise nature of Wotan's sin? The answer to this question depends on the two-dimensional aspect of Alberich's original action as distinguished above. The initial and obvious response is that Wotan's sin is theft. Wotan has been advised to steal what Alberich has himself stolen. In general, it is obvious that if *A* steals something, this immoral act hardly justifies *B*'s stealing that something from *A*. *A* himself has no right to what he now possesses because its possession was obtained by theft. But *B* is no less a thief simply because what he takes from *A* has itself been stolen. Therefore, Alberich legitimately refers to Wotan as a robber and a thief, both at the time of Wotan's original seizure of the gold and later when the two meet in the second act of *Siegfried*.

No one would deny that theft is a serious offense. But is theft so serious that it warrants the ferocity of Alberich's cry that the thief Wotan will sin against everything that "was, is, and will be"? The answer, I suggest, is no, if (*a*) the second dimension of Alberich's original action and (*b*) what Wotan intended to achieve by his subsequent theft of the golden ring are both taken into account. Notice that Alberich's anger reaches fever pitch only when Wotan threatens to steal the ring, not when Wotan announces his intention to procure the golden treasure as such. Alberich realizes that the treasure can always be refashioned, since the power to attain such palpable ends emanates from possession of the ring. However, once Alberich loses the ring, he loses the power attached to the ring. Alberich's anger is therefore directed both at the act of stealing itself and at the loss of the object which the thief Wotan now possesses. What has been stolen is the ring. And Alberich won the right to the magical charms which allowed the Rhinegold to be forged into the ring not by the act of stealing the Rhinegold as such, but only after he foreswore love for power.

As a thief, Alberich gave up nothing when he wrested the Rhinegold from the protection of the Rhinemaidens. In general, of course, theft would lose its attractiveness if the potential thief knew in advance that he would have to give up something of value equivalent or perhaps even greater than that which he intended to steal. However, once in possession of the gold, Alberich certainly has to give up something of value to himself, his failures at love notwithstanding. In a very real sense, Alberich's exchange of love for power is a contractual event on the same fundamental level as when Wotan exchanged partial sight for the wisdom and power to guard the world. In fact, Alberich's sacrifice was far more emasculating to self than Wotan's, for partial blindness is surely less severe a handicap than life without love. But Alberich's greater hardship only underscores the justifiable reason for his wrathful denunciation. Alberich is not angry at Wotan simply because Wotan stole Alberich's ring; he is angry because Wotan has stolen the ring, thinking that he, Wotan, can avail himself of the ring's power *without having to fulfill the required contractual exchange,* in this case renouncing one desired end for another desired end, i.e., love for power.

Wotan is a thief, to be sure. But I suggest that Wotan's real sin is the willful disruption of the contract that Alberich has entered. This action—and not mere theft—is that action which sins against "what was, is, and will be." One may wonder whether Wotan intended to sin against the institution of contracts in the same way that he obviously intended to become a thief. The text of the poem provides a reliable answer. Shortly after Loge had advised Wotan to steal the ring, both Loge and Froh observed—with Wotan listening carefully—that the ring may now be carried off without the new possessor of the ring bearing the burden presently shouldered by Alberich. The ignoble dwarf had been willing to foreswear love, a condition to which the deity Wotan, in his regal lust, would never consent. Therefore, Wotan knows that if he acquires the ring, he need not fear incurring the responsibility now borne by Alberich. Since Wotan does steal the ring, it may be assumed that he does so, at least in part, precisely because he knows that this particularly inhibiting contractual condition is no longer operative. Both the exalted Wotan and the base Alberich exist in a world order that requires that contracts be made and, once made, that they be complied with. Wotan was or should have been more acutely aware of this fact than anyone else, but his conduct toward Alberich (as well as his earlier conduct toward the giants) scarcely befits the guardian of all contracts and oaths. Alberich immediately senses Wotan's failure and cries out against the wrong done, not simply to himself as an individual, but to a world that is ordered on the sacred character of such contractual exchanges.

An unwise contract and Wotan's subsequent attempt to renege on it were the immediate causes of his present predicament with Alberich. Also, evidence to indicate that Wotan may well have already violated the contractual character of his own marital oath was earlier examined. The theft of the ring and the violation of the contract that engendered that ring finally release a force of power for evil consequences that Wotan's problems with earlier contracts had only foreshadowed. If the legitimacy of Wotan's world rule depends on the guardianship of contracts, it would be naive on Wotan's part to assume that concerted violations of the contractual bond with apparent impunity would not have an ultimately dire effect on his rule. Should the powers of nature that originally sanctioned Wotan's regime be as jealous as the Old Testament deity, then the very first occurrence of improper conduct with respect to contracts—regardless of who is involved—may have necessarily resulted in Wotan's eventual downfall. It is known that Wotan is explicitly involved in a series of contractual violations. This involvement suggests that no single episode can be designated as *the* fateful moment in his career. Wotan's moral decay is gradual but irreversible, just as the course of events leading to his demise is slow but inexorable.

There is, nonetheless, special significance to the confrontation between Wotan and Alberich and to Wotan's disruption of Alberich's contractual exchange of love for power. Wotan achieved power sufficient to guard the world after drinking from nature's spring. Alberich also desires power to rule the world, and he rips the gold from the Rhine as a necessary prerequisite for its possession. Thus, the power possessed by Wotan is to the power desired by Alberich (and Wotan himself) as the peaceful spring is to the mighty Rhine. There are two reasons that suggest that the power tapped by Alberich possesses more potency than the power that substantiates Wotan's present rule. First, and obvious, is the fact that Wotan desires that power even though he already has more power than anyone else. It follows that the measure of power desired must exceed the measure of power possessed, for if it were less or even equivalent, there would be no reason for Wotan to desire it. Second, Alberich takes revenge on Wotan's theft of the ring by cursing the ring. Events show that the power behind this curse will destroy Wotan and his regime; therefore, this power must be greater than the power which once grounded that regime. By usurping the golden ring, Wotan came into direct conflict with one who had assumed the awesome burden of directing power sufficient for world domination. Whether Alberich would or would not have succeeded in his quest is irrelevant. The point is that Alberich's contractual acquisition of the golden ring is based on immediate contact with the source of power greater than any power so far exercised.

It is known that the ultimate source of Wotan's power is nature and it may be safely inferred that the ultimate source of Alberich's (potential) power is also nature via the gold as a natural element. Thus, the difference between Alberich's power and Wotan's power is one of degree and not of kind, since the source of power is the same in each case. The contracts binding Wotan to the giants and to Fricka, contracts engineered by virtue of the conditions that originally granted power to Wotan, were derivative in that they concerned ends based on the specific and restricted interests of the parties involved. Wotan's failure to abide by the letter of these contracts is, at the time, harmful to him in a manner commensurate with their derivative character. But Alberich's contractual exchange is for control of the kind of power that established the very possibility of these and all other forms of contracts. Therefore, Alberich's contract is of an especially fundamental sort. When Wotan interferes with this contract, he knowingly and willingly sins against the source of the power for which Alberich thirsts. But since the source of Alberich's power is the same as the source of his own power, Wotan in effect sins against the source which sanctions Wotan's own contracts and, of course, against the legitimacy of his own regime. Therefore, in his pursuit of power even greater than that which he already possessed, Wotan could not help but destroy himself, since he intentionally violated the very institution that presented him with power in the first place.

Alberich without the ring is, in a sense, a much more formidable enemy than Alberich with the ring. He retaliates against the severity of Wotan's sin by uttering a curse. And the letter of the curse once again reveals the contractual character that defined his original acquisition of the ring:

> Wie durch Fluch er mir geriet,
> verflucht sei dieser Ring!
>
> (As it came to me through a curse,
> So may this ring be accursed!)

Alberich clearly indicates that he himself was cursed, not by reason of the theft of the Rhinegold, but in the subsequent contractual exchange of love for power that allowed him to forge the Rhinegold into the ring. No curse has been placed on either love or power as such. Rather, the curse concerns a relation between love and power, since the curse comes into effect only when one barters away the blandishments of love for the sake of acquiring power.

Two inferences are worth noting at this point. Both are relatively abstract, and their introduction here momentarily shifts the critical perspective away from the immediacy of the *Ring* as such. But they are the kind of abstraction that must eventually be considered before the immediacy of the *Ring* can be transmuted into a comprehensive understanding of the meaning of that immediacy. To mention them now may keep this requirement fresh in mind. First, if Alberich's exchange of love for power is cursed by the very nature of the contract, then perhaps Wotan's original exchange of natural vision for natural wisdom and power was similarly cursed. This possibility suggests an objective hierarchy of values, a natural law of values such that a choice for the lower rather than the higher value "curses" the chooser to an evil or at least unhappy end. Second, if the curse on Alberich is universal in form, applicable to any individual who gives up love for power, then this stricture must be indicative of the relative status of love and power, i.e., that love always surpasses power in terms of ultimate importance. This possibility suggests how the hierarchy of values is ordered, at least with respect to two of the members of that hierarchy. Whether or not these inferences are sound, or are even amenable to resolution, is, however, a matter best left to the retrospect in chapter 3.

For now, it is certain that nature has dictated the appropriateness of a curse, given that the wizened Alberich has contractually sacrificed love for power and then has lost the right to pursue and exercise power as a result of Wotan's illicit intervention in that contract. Furthermore, the fact that the curse arises in the way that it does reveals the presence of a climactic conflict, not between individuals as such, but between values of crucial significance. This conflict, posed early in what Wagner intended to be the prologue to the *Ring*, establishes a background setting for many of the interpersonal conflicts which define subsequent events in the *Ring* proper. The conflict is love versus power, a conflict which is certainly not necessitated by the intrinsic nature of these two realities. For, on the face of things, love and power need never be opposed to one another. One can pursue love and be completely uninterested in power, or one can pursue power and be completely uninterested in love. And, of course, one could pursue love and power simultaneously and be perfectly successful in both endeavors. But the curse activated by Alberich in effect fuses love and power from this point on until the *Ring* reaches its apotheosis. Regardless of whether a character attempts to win love or to attain power, regardless of the sincerity of that love or the rightness of that quest for power, the fate of that character will be affected by the fact that both love and power have become infected by a curse. Although the immediate context of the curse includes only Alberich and Wotan, the extent of the curse's malignancy is as pervasive as the full range of characters who must live and struggle in the shadow of that curse. It may be concluded that if, in general, love and power are affected in such a dire way by the forces behind a dwarf's imprecation, then it would perhaps be wise to suspect that the very institution of contracts itself can be similarly affected.

At the point at which Alberich utters the curse, he has been denied both the ring and all that he had acquired by virtue of its possession. What then is the precise source of the power that substantiates his curse? The answer may be found by reflecting on the fact that Alberich does not curse the gold, nor does he curse Wotan—rather, he curses the ring. The ring itself is a tangible product of an intangible act: Alberich's contractual exchange of love for power. The fact that Alberich no longer possesses the physical presence of the ring affects Alberich only in the sense that the positive powers latent in the ring have been reduced to negative deterrents. *But the contractual exchange between Alberich and nature that permitted Alberich to forge the ring remains in force.* It remains in force just as Wotan's contract with the giants was binding (even though Wotan had no intention of keeping that contract when he made it), and just as the marital oath between Hunding and Sieglinde was binding (even though Siegmund and Sieglinde's passionate love seemed to Wotan good reason to ignore its violation). While Alberich can no longer personally wield the power accruing from that contract for his own self-interest, he retains the capacity to direct that power so that whoever attempts to exercise it in his stead should suffer from the attempt. Alberich becomes the guide for the ring's power, since it is his act of will that dictates that possession of the ring should result in evil rather than good for its possessor. It is not accidental that Wagner refers to the ring as "Alberich's ring" in later music dramas.[5] By right, or until certain other conditions have been fulfilled, the ring remains Alberich's regardless of who may subsequently have it in his or her possession.

The power of the ring does not, therefore, emanate from Alberich, who merely channels that power, but from the contractual exchange to which Alberich has consented and from which he may, with complete justification, anticipate self-advantageous benefits. One overlooks the deeper significance of Alberich's "curse" if it is construed as merely an aesthetic throwback to grand operatic tradition. At a more fundamental level, the curse may be seen as a verbalized symbol in which are collected all the evil repercussions consequent upon the misuse and abuse of contracts. To contract for power at the price of sacrificing love may, in the end, prove to be unwise by the very nature of things. Nonetheless, the institutional device that sanctioned that exchange remains in force. I suggest that the source of the power that substantiates Alberich's curse can be located and explained only on this basis. And the evil effects of the curse will be more than apparent in the events to follow. Although those who will seek the ring are almost exclusively concerned with the acquisition of power, an end that in itself is morally neutral, the concrete application of the ring in pursuit of that end will consistently result in deception, disgrace, treachery, and death. The cursed ring generates a measure of evil equivalent to, perhaps even greater than, the measure of good bestowed on the world by Wotan's original exchange of partial vision for natural wisdom.

I conclude on a reflective note. Alberich and Wotan are polar opposites in many respects. Alberich is an ugly dwarf; Wotan is a royal deity. Alberich lives in a refurbished cave; Wotan lives in a resplendent castle. Alberich lacks love; Wotan has been glutted with love. When Alberich does achieve a modicum of power, he rules a kingdom of dwarves deep in the bowels of the earth; Wotan's power is exercised over the gods in the heavens and over all mortals throughout the farthest reaches of the earth. Such universal opposition suggests that Alberich and Wotan represent, in a sense, the limits of consciousness. However, given that Alberich is a dwarf and that Wotan is a deity, can these limits be equated to the limits of *human* consciousness? The answer is surely yes. Alberich and Wotan are ultimately as human as any of the strictly human characters of the *Ring*. The fact that neither of these limits is presented by a specifically human character suggests that however high man may aspire or however low he may sink, man will continue to be defined by certain natural strengths and weaknesses. And, in the present set of circumstances, these strengths and weaknesses are specified through a conflict in which the opposition between dwarf and deity becomes compressed into one kind of interpersonal relation. Alberich and Wotan first meet only because Wotan must fulfill a contract; Alberich departs only after Alberich curses Wotan's ring because Wotan has violated a contract that Alberich has fulfilled. Thus, the arena in which the various oppositions between Alberich and Wotan will be resolved is located within boundaries set by the institution of contracts. At the conclusion of this phase of their confrontation, the dwarf has the upper hand over the deity by virtue of the cursed ring now in the deity's possession. The forces of base consciousness have begun to waste away the already weakened powers of exalted consciousness.

The Wanderer and Mime

At the conclusion of *Die Walküre*, just before he invoked Loge to surround Brünnhilde's rock with fire, Wotan had announced that he must go "far away" (*Doch fort muss ich jetzt, / fern von dir zieh'n*). Wotan becomes a Wanderer, just as his mortal son Siegmund wandered far and wide before finding himself at the hearth of Hunding's hut. The wandering condition of the son of a divinity is now mirrored by the wandering of that divinity himself. But why does Wotan feel constrained to wander? In the previous section, I presented reasons indicating why Wotan's position as guardian of the world was in peril. In the subsequent section, which considers the Wanderer and Siegfried and the events surrounding Wotan's dethronement, I shall offer additional reasons why Wotan must undergo this peripatetic period. But, as will now be seen, Wotan the Wanderer's confrontation with Mime forms an important bridge spanning the events discussed in these two sections, especially with respect to Wotan's connection with the institution of contracts.

When Wotan appears before Mime in the first act of *Siegfried*, his identity is synonymous with his present condition: "The world calls me Wanderer" (*Wanderer heisst mich die Welt*). Mime, dwarfishly clever but not overly perceptive, readily intuits the Wanderer's real identity, so other mortal observers have doubtless perceived it as well. A wanderer of unknown identity is one thing, but a Wanderer who is really Wotan is quite another matter. Thus, Wotan's transformation from ruler to wanderer has received the greatest possible notoriety. And his actions as Wanderer testify to the democratic scope of this condition, for he tells Mime that during his wanderings he has aided many individuals who had thought themselves wise. However, one must wonder whether the wisdom of a deity now publicly

named by his wandering condition is real, vestigial, or merely sham.
Wagner's stage directions reinforce this suspicion. The Wanderer is garbed
with a hat that slouches over his "lacking" (*fehlende*) eye. Since Wotan is
already blind in one eye, the Wanderer is, so to speak, in double darkness, as
if the artifical vesture camouflaging his sightless eye reflected in some
important way the acquisition of those contracts which originally caused his
real partial blindness.

The Wanderer approaches Mime's dwelling and requests the hospitality of
the hearth. The dwarf Mime, beset by problems with the hero Siegfried and
with his own ambition, is in no mood for the amenities. One notes first the
instructive parallel between the Wanderer's entrance in *Siegfried* and
Wotan's entrance in *Das Rheingold*. In *Das Rheingold*, Wotan, at the height
of his power, has just contracted for the construction of a castle in which he
can live and rule in the regal resplendence appropriate for the king of gods
and men. But in *Siegfried*, Wotan has been reduced to a wanderer seeking
temporary lodgings in a cave inhabited by a dwarf. Nevertheless, even access
to these mean surroundings requires that the Wanderer must challenge
Mime to a "wager" (*Wette*) of knowledge, on which wager the Wanderer
stakes his head as "pledge" (*Pfand*). Thus, the Wanderer must wager to rest
in Mime's cave, just as Wotan was compelled to contract for the luxury of
Valhalla. The squalor of the cave is to the glory of Valhalla as the hollowness of
the wager for access to the cave is to the holiness of the contract for
construction of the castle.

The wager has its due conditions: Mime will ask the Wanderer three
questions, and the Wanderer will then do the same. Mime guarantees the
Wanderer hospitality in exchange for knowledge that Mime hopes will be
useful to him. If the Wanderer does not provide such knowledge, his head is
forfeit. If, in turn, Mime cannot answer the Wanderer's questions, he also is
subject to the same deadly loss.

It is not accidental, I believe, that the structure of this wager duplicates all
the formal characteristics of a contract. And since the contract leitmotif is
heard several times in the orchestra while the conditions of the wager are
discussed by the participants, it is appropriate from both the verbal and the
musical perspectives to construe the wager as a specific kind of contract,
although in a somewhat disguised form. As the wager is resolved, the
Wanderer and Mime repeat many important details of past events in the
Ring, and it has become almost axiomatic to categorize the wager episode as
a dramatic device that dispenses information in order to refresh the collective
memory of the audience. But this critical judgment overemphasizes content
at the expense of form, so much so that an important aspect of the episode is
overlooked. The contractual form of the wager episode is as vital to the
thought structure of the *Ring* as the content revealed during that episode.
The pledge (*Pfand*) for Valhalla was Freia, the source of the gods' youth; the

pledge (*Pfand*) for the relative comfort of Mime's hearth is the Wanderer's head. In both cases, Wotan's contracts are based on conditions of payment that are fundamental in every respect. We have seen what happened when Wotan reneged on the first pledge; his actions with respect to the second pledge may be equally fateful.

After he successfully answers Mime's third question, the Wanderer strikes the ground with his spear; according to Wagner's staging, "a soft stroke of thunder" sounds (*ein leiser Donner*). This gesture is important for two reasons: the thunder indicates that even though Wotan has become a wanderer, he still retains a vestige of power; but the softness of the thunder signals that this power rapidly diminishes, that the connection between wooden spear and natural forces has become severely weakened. The fact that Wotan as the Wanderer retains his former regal status to the point of wielding the spear and exercising that power, however slight it may now be, is nonetheless significant. But, although he retains a semblance of real power, the Wanderer's replies in the course of fulfilling his end of the wager implicitly denote the state to which he has descended. His answer to Mime's question concerning the nature of the race that dwells in the lofty heights of heaven is couched in the third person. Wotan the Wanderer discourses about Wotan the guardian of the world as if the two were distinct. And in a very real sense they are distinct. The Wanderer's subsequent testimony indicates the reason for this usual gap between aspects of the same personality. Although records of "holy contracts" (*Heil'ger Verträge*) are notched on the Wanderer's spear, this part of the spear "withers" (*dorrt*) while the "point" (*Spitze*) of the spear remains intact. At least part of the purpose of Wotan's wandering quest may now be disclosed: as the Wanderer, he wants somehow to preserve the power symbolized by the point of the spear in the face of the knowledge that the spear's shaft is as withered as the contractual bonds that once elevated him as Wotan to a position of highest authority. The shaft may be little more than a stick, but Mime still quakes before the point of that spear. Later in the drama, Siegfried will not quake.

The Wanderer readily satisfies his end of the wager, but only because Mime is more concerned to rebuff the Wanderer than to pursue his own self-interest. He fails to question the Wanderer concerning what had heretofore been uppermost in his mind, the technique required to forge the sword necessary to win the golden treasure now in the possession of the dormant dragon Fafner. The dwarf Mime is not wise in his questions while pursuing the ring, just as his brother dwarf Alberich was not wise in his actions when he actually did possess it. Thus, when the time comes for Mime to answer the Wanderer's questions, Mime has lost his advantage and fails to answer precisely that problem when it is posed by the Wanderer, i.e., how to forge the pieces of the sword.

Mime is now beholden to the Wanderer, for the wager has been resolved in the Wanderer's favor. Although the figure of the Wanderer retains a certain majesty in this confrontation, it is majesty produced by the comparative baseness of the surroundings rather than from any intrinsic nobility on the Wanderer's part. In fact, the actions of Wotan the Wanderer after the termination of the wager indicate both the present status of the institution of contracts and Wotan's wandering relation to that institution. If, as suggested above, this wager, as all wagers, is a species of contract, then strictly speaking the Wanderer should have taken Mime's head. By the Wanderer's own admission, a wager entails an "obligation" (*Pflicht*) to fulfill its conditions, presumably an obligation that applies universally, even to wandering deities. But the Wanderer does not take Mime's head; instead, he proclaims that the disposition of Mime's head will be left to "one who has not learned fear" (*der das Fürchten nicht gelernt*). The Wanderer then disappears, laughing, into the forest outside Mime's cave.

The Wanderer's laughter at the outcome of the wager reflects the fact that a wager between deity and dwarf is a virtual parody of the high seriousness of the contractual structure on which that wager is based. Furthermore, the Wanderer's sudden departure is also significant if viewed as a deviation from the contractual norm. There are, of course, important dramatic reasons why Mime's head must remain intact until the end of act 2, reasons that obviously could not be advanced should the Wanderer exact that pledge at this point in act 1. However, the relevant point in this context does not concern Mime's future fate, but rather the reason why the Wanderer acts as he does in the present.

The Wanderer does not take Mime's head, but the Wanderer does know who is capable of taking Mime's head, i.e., one who has not yet learned fear. The hero Siegfried has not yet learned fear, and there is every reason to believe that the Wanderer is fully aware that Siegfried possesses this characteristic. Therefore, we may safely assume that the Wanderer knows who will eventually dispose of Mime. By postponing the exactment of what is his and by stipulating who will be his contractual representative (as it were), Wotan the Wanderer subtly but effectively binds Siegfried to Wotan the one-time resplendent ruler of Valhalla. Siegfried then becomes an unknowing agent in a contractual wager originally taking place between the Wanderer and Mime. And when Siegfried does dispatch Mime, he completes the contractual conditions of this wager. Siegfried has become, in a very real sense, the Wanderer's right arm. To delegate a representative in a contractual exchange is hardly an improper act. But the original perpetrator of this particular contract knows that his position—depending for its legitimacy on the sacredness of the institution of contracts—has become all but impossible precisely by virtue of violations directed at that very institution. As a result, the Wanderer's seemingly harmless delegation of the wager's fulfillment to Siegfried shows how far Wotan has wandered from the source of wisdom and power. Wotan desperately needs the services of a free hero. However, Wotan the Wanderer's conduct after his successful wager with Mime effectively shackles Siegfried (the only hero available) to the same moribund institution which compelled Wotan's need for a hero in the first place.

The wager between the Wanderer and Mime becomes a beacon illuminating past, present, and future. This wager looks back to Wotan's more important but essentially illicit contracts, highlights the present shattered state of contracts in general, and glances forward to the Wanderer's imminent meeting with Siegfried, when the shaft of the divine spear will be split in two by a human agent who does not really know what he is doing. The spear has decayed into a harmless stick from improper use of what it symbolizes, just as Wotan has been reduced from guardian of the world to a wanderer in that world. The unfulfilled status of the wager underscores the extent of Wotan's present hollowness as well as the present sterility of the institution by which he once so grandly ruled.

The Wanderer and Siegfried

In the third act of *Siegfried,* the hero Siegfried brandishes the sword Nothung and splinters the Wanderer's spear into two pieces. Just prior to Siegfried's deed, the Wanderer refers to his weapon as his "eternal spear" (*ewigen Speer*). But of course it is not eternal, as Siegfried quickly demonstrates. The spear recording Wotan's legitimacy has finally been destroyed. Retrieving the pieces of the broken spear, the Wanderer departs, saying to himself as much as to Siegfried:

> Zieh hin! Ich kann dich nicht halten!
>
> (Go on! I cannot stop you!)

It is learned later in *Götterdämmerung* that the Wanderer returned to Valhalla and resumed his role as Wotan, but as Wotan stripped of divine power and authority. He sits, broods, ages, and waits for the inevitable.

Since Wotan does not appear again in the *Ring,* the event that finalizes his departure from the world he once ruled must be carefully examined, beginning with the fact that Wotan as the Wanderer freely chose to take a stand in his own defense. Clearly, the Wanderer hoped that the spear could be wielded against Siegfried with the same force and effect as it had been against Siegmund in *Die Walküre.* Events prove that this hope is unwarranted. But the relevant point is that he intended to exercise the power granted to him by virtue of what the spear represented. This intention presupposes that the Wanderer believed that the spear's power was still available to him, as it had always been available to him, and that it could and should be used to protect his regime. But, as will be seen, this presupposition conflicts with beliefs expressed by Wotan in two important previous episodes. Exploring this conflict will help to discern the principal reasons behind the Wanderer's mixed motivation and to understand more completely the complex significance of Siegfried's action.

The key episodes circumscribing the conflict between the Wanderer's defensive tactics and Wotan's prior beliefs occur, respectively, in (a) the long conversation with Brünnhilde in the second act of *Die Walküre* and in (b) the shorter exchange with Erda in the third act of *Siegfried*.

(a) Wotan reveals to Brünnhilde that should the evil Alberich regain possession of the ring and then attack Valhalla, the demise of the gods will be guaranteed, a fate that Wotan judges to be an "endless shame" (*endloser Schmach*). Wotan, warned earlier by Erda of the dangers attached to the ring, has fathered Brünnhilde and the other eight Valkyries to procure heroic warriors and thus aid in providing protection for himself. At this point, the ring is hoarded as part of the golden treasure by the giant Fafner, now transformed by the Tarnhelm into a comatose dragon. But Wotan cannot help himself or the other gods by forcibly seizing the ring from Fafner, a deed that is expressly "forbidden" (*verwehrt*) to the gods. It is forbidden not by any lack of divine power, but because Wotan is not allowed to strike one with whom he had made a contract.

In the guise of a fierce and nameless mortal warrior, Wotan had attempted to circumvent this restriction by siring a son by a mortal woman, a man of heroic dimension who would not know his father's divine identity and who, by his own free choice, would eventually act to insure that the ring not fall into the hands of those who would unseat the gods. This man is Siegmund. But Siegmund, acting according to primeval dictates of blood and passion, loves Sieglinde. Although their meeting is, according to Siegmund, "decreed" (*bestimmt*), their subsequent illicit union sparks the wrath of Fricka, guardian of the marital oath. Fricka charges Wotan to protect that contractual bond and to avenge the lovers' sinful union. Wotan, heartsore at the prospective destruction of his own offspring, cannot escape the stricture of contracts, either his own (with the giants) or those which by right he must protect (the marital oath). In a strikingly taut antithesis, he laments to Brünnhilde:

> der durch Verträge ich Herr;
> den Verträgen bin ich nun Knecht.
>
> (I, master by virtue of contracts,
> am now a slave to them.)

Wotan concludes that "only one thing more do I will—the end! the end!" His bitterness at having to endure the "hollow pomp of divinity" (*der Gottheit nichtigen Glanz*) is without limits; in a word, his sadness is "eternal" (*ew'ge*).

If the divine regime cannot be saved by Wotan's own efforts, then that regime does not merit salvation. For that deity in charge of all other deities, salvation by chance—by the act of a human agent unaware of its cosmic importance—is not salvation at all.

But at this point tension arises between what Wotan says here and what Wotan the Wanderer does later. For if Wotan is sincere in willing the end of the gods now in *Die Walküre*, why should he exercise the instrument of power in defense of the gods later in *Siegfried?*

(b) A close similarity exists between Wotan's attitude toward his regime as described in (a) and the attitude expressed in *Siegfried* just prior to his climactic meeting with that drama's hero. Whereas in *Die Walküre* Wotan was fearful of the threat posed by Alberich, Wotan the Wanderer tells Alberich face to face that the dwarf's destructive intention no longer "causes him care" (*sorgt*). Wotan's spear of contracts cannot be used against Alberich, as the dwarf shrewdly notes, but the Wanderer nonetheless believes that the spear retains its power (*Kraft*) and is therefore worth preserving, especially in time of war. However, if the Wanderer is sincere in his avowed preparations for war, this sincerity presupposes that he intends to act forcefully to preserve the race of gods. The strength of this intention is reinforced during his meeting with Erda at the beginning of the third act. The Wanderer, resting on his spear while hailing Erda, asks her "how to halt a turning wheel" (*wie zu hemmen ein rollendes Rad*). The implication seems to be that if Erda can provide the Wanderer with information to halt or even to brake the course of events, the Wanderer would take advantage of that information for precisely the attainment of that end. However, the Wanderer had told Alberich at the beginning of the second act that "I came to watch, not to act" (*Zu schauen kam ich, / nicht zu schaffen*). And this claim implies that *any* action on his part, martial or otherwise, would be otiose in view of the fact that all events are completely determined. Furthermore, shortly before Erda vanishes into the earth, the Wanderer exclaims that "joyfully and gladly" (*froh und freudig*) he now "freely" (*frei*) embraces what heretofore he had envisioned only with the deepest despair and pain: the "end of the gods" (*der Götter Ende*). The Wanderer also senses, in a moment of prescience, that he is about to confront Siegfried, before whom Alberich's curse is impotent, and he tells Erda that he will grow weak "in joy" (*in Wonne*) before that eternal youth.

The same question introduced at the end of (a) must also be raised here: If the Wanderer gladly and joyfully wills the end of the gods, if he anticipates the arrival of Siegfried with a unique form of ecstasy, why does he attempt to defend himself and his regime at Siegfried's expense when their confrontation actually occurs? Juxtaposing the acceptance of his fate and the defense against that fate sets in relief what Wotan was in the past, as sketched in (a) and (b) above, and what Wotan the Wanderer is now. For during his abortive struggle with Siegfried, a classic study in intense and dramatic self-conflict takes place. The principal combatants in this conflict are the Wanderer's knowledge of a future world without Wotan as guardian and his desire, fueled by the simple fact that he continues to exist, to preserve the tradition if not the glory of his past regime.

The Wanderer's knowledge that the world will go on without him is based on the fact that, to paraphrase his own lament, he is a slave to the very contracts that had once made him master. The immediate causes of this servitude may be outlined as follows: In order to meet a contractual agreement with the giants—a dubious enterprise in itself—Wotan had to interfere with a contract Alberich had made with the source of the Rhinegold's power. Then, to extricate himself from the resulting threat to the gods, he had to break his own marital oath to Fricka in order to sire Siegmund. And, finally, he had to permit the violation of the marital oath between Sieglinde and Hunding in order that a hero be engendered by the union of Siegmund and Sieglinde. Wotan knows that he has been guilty of all these offences against the principle of his own legitimacy and he knows this fact before he asserts, both in *Die Walküre* and in *Siegfried*, that he wills the end of the gods. Whatever the means by which servitude is impressed, a god reduced to slavery is a god in name only. In this case, Wotan's desire for self-destruction may be seen as an inevitable consequence of his self-acknowledged unworthiness to guard a world based on and ordered by contracts, especially in view of the fact that the most destructive conduct toward contracts, both his own and others, has originated with Wotan himself.

Wotan's realization of his fate and of the causal process underlying that fate reaches its full intensity at the conclusion of *Die Walküre*, when he announces that he must begin to wander the earth. In *Siegfried*, he explains further that he had to wander in order to search for whatever wisdom could be derived from the world and its affairs. The transition from Wotan the divine ruler who senses his fate to Wotan the Wanderer is a form of consummation in which the knowledge that his regime was doomed becomes fused with the active gathering of all worldly wisdom to himself. Assuming that Siegfried is less than thirty years old when slain by Hagen, this internal evidence implies that Wotan's period of wandering lasted up to thirty years, from the time immediately after Brünnhilde is confined to her rock of fire to the moment when Wotan the Wanderer confronts the youthful hero. Once this lengthy period devoted to action was completed, the Wanderer collected in his person and in its entirety both the theoretical and the practical dimensions of wisdom in that world which the royal deity once guarded. As the Wanderer becomes filled with wisdom, Erda—the primeval mouthpiece for the source of that wisdom—becomes drained of it; hence her drowsy condition when the two meet in the third act of *Siegfried*. The Wanderer invokes her presence, not just so that she may provide him with the means to halt what is necessary, as hypothesized above, but also to announce that Erda herself is fated to expire. Those little reserves of her wisdom not yet gathered by the wisdom-seeking Wanderer will become like the dust of cremation, or, perhaps more apt, like the ashes of Valhalla.

The transition from Wotan's care and fear (*Das Rheingold*) to Wotan's pain (*Die Walküre*) to the Wanderer's joy (*Siegfried*) serves as an emotional mirror reflecting the transition from Wotan the ruler in search of a way to save his regime to Wotan the Wanderer in anticipation of a new principle of order. Fear, an emotion directly related to the future during which the fear will prove founded or unfounded, is also related to the past, in those instances when some recognizable cause of the fear can be discerned. In this case, Wotan's fear is occasioned by a past contract that has compelled him to act in direct violation of the institution of contracts. As a result, Wotan fears that his rule will decrease in scope and duration, perhaps even vanish altogether. Pain is an emotion necessarily experienced in the present. Remembered pain and anticipated pain are not themselves painful experiences, at least not in the way that the original experiences were or will be painful. Wotan's pain is the inevitable outcome of his fear, thus gathering the past into the present. Wotan now knows—and senses—the repercussions of his past actions, especially all the contractual abuses. Finally, Wotan's fear and pain are collected and then transformed into joy. But why joy, an emotion experienced in the actual presence of something rather than in its future possibility? Wotan looks to the end of the gods with joy because he has become aware that what had once been fresh and alive in the past has now decayed and will be transmuted into something new and vital in the future. Whatever has been inhibited by the constrictive force of contracts and oaths will then be free to grow and flourish. These three phases in Wotan's emotional spectrum thus generate a virtual compression of time within the presence of contracts: fear—from past unwise contracts; pain—from the present repercussions of these contracts; joy—from the realization of future freedom from contracts of this sort.

This temporal perspective adds an important dimension in explaining the Wanderer's struggle against Siegfried. Why, it may be asked, did the Wanderer not simply embrace the joy to which he attests and then graciously abdicate? I suggest that a complete answer to this question depends on recognizing the relation between the emotions displayed by Wotan in these contractual contexts and the nature of time as such. Every epoch in world history must run its allotted course. The *Ring* presents an account of one such epoch. Wotan's epoch was inaugurated by an act of violence and self-mutilation. As a result of this act, he received both wisdom and power, constituted symbolically by the sharply-pointed spear engraved with contracts. But now, at the conclusion of this epoch, it would run contrary to tradition for Wotan to depart without some form of physical struggle. Even a warrior god who now knows that his future is doomed must meet that doom in a manner befitting his past nature. If he does not, he forfeits all hope of retaining even a semblance of honor in future epochs. The wisdom and power of an entire era has been collected in the Wanderer and his spear, and in every essential respect that union is all but dead. But as long as the union remains, even if only as a shell without underlying substance, no fresh ground breaking for the new order can take place.

Given this temporal perspective, the Wanderer's personal struggle, both emotionally within himself and militarily against Siegfried, can be viewed as the final necessity in the violent transition from one epoch to another. The struggle between representatives of the old and the new is all the more noteworthy for its brevity. In an instant, Siegfried's vibrant sword shatters the Wanderer's brittle spear. The Wanderer himself remains unharmed, but the destruction of his now mortal form is only postponed until the fiery purgation of Valhalla. In fact, before departing in defeat, Wotan the Wanderer collects the pieces of his once-potent spear; they will serve as relics of his rule while he awaits the final holocaust. Neither the corpse of a fallen deity nor the remnants of his broken spear will disfigure the purity of an earth now waiting for a revitalized source of power and authority. Siegfried's destruction of the spear of contracts seals Wotan's destiny, regardless of what subsequently happens to Valhalla. The fiery holocaust that consumes Valhalla and its divine denizens only recapitulates in a spectacularly public form the implicit consequences following from the momentous confrontation in the third act of *Siegfried*.

Siegfried, the victor in this epochal confrontation, has been referred to by Wotan as the "eternal youth." But the heroic Siegfried is hardly eternal. Hagen's treachery in *Götterdämmerung* will testify to the fact that, despite his apparent bravery, Siegfried is quite mortal. As far as Wotan is concerned, the reference to Siegfried's supposed divinity denotes a new principle of life and order, as uncorrupted by illicit and unfulfilled contracts as Siegfried is by the curse that Alberich invoked because of one such violated contract. The Wanderer "cannot stop" the advent of this epoch with its new principle of order, just as he cannot halt its individual and heroic herald.

But what can the cryptic reference to eternity mean with respect to Siegfried himself? I suggest that the epithet "eternal youth" carefully juxtaposes both the strength and weakness of Seigfried. As noted, Siegfried is immune to the cursed ring because he has never willfully become entangled in the contractual restrictions that led to the imposition of that curse. In general, youth and innocence go hand in hand, and Siegfried's innocence in this respect is further attested to by the fact that even with the ring in his possession, he still does not know of the ring's capacity for bestowing power. Nor is there any evidence to suggest that he would be interested in world domination. When, during his sportive session with the Rhinemaidens,

Siegfried does learn the details of the curse on the ring, he remains under the effects of Hagen's magic potion; however, even in this state he does not act as if the acquisition of power was at all significant to him. The youthful Siegfried can therefore be seen as a source of eternal hope and optimism for the future.

Nevertheless, however innocent Siegfried may be of the ring's seductive lure, his eternal youth remains bound by the inherent taint of Wotan's lineage. Siegfried is the son of Siegmund and Sieglinde, who in turn are the progeny of Wotan. Thus, Siegfried is Wotan's grandson. Furthermore, the Wanderer has already told Erda that Siegfried has been "chosen by me" (*von mir erkoren*), just as Siegfried's father had been chosen. But although the Wanderer can claim with justification to have *chosen* Siegfried to play a divinely appointed role, the Wanderer does not claim to have *compelled* Siegfried actually to play that role. This distinction both shows how freedom from the old tradition is embodied in Seigfried and also helps to explain why Wotan the Wanderer departs from his defeat at the hands of Siegfried in considerable anguish. Wotan has chosen this hero, but the hero need not have, in turn, chosen that course of action which Wotan himself both hoped for and feared. The fact that Siegfried did so choose is the final crushing blow to Wotan's regime and its erstwhile leader, both now wandering on the brink of extinction.

At this climactic moment in history, Siegfried is as young as Wotan is old. But the youthful embodiment of everything epochally new and vital will himself die in the very flower of his youth. Presumably one reason for Siegfried's death in such circumstances lies in his unavoidable proximity to the institution of contracts. Siegfried's birth and life are, after all, spent entirely in the sphere of Wotan's influence. But, whatever may be the full cause, it remains true that Siegfried's youth did not attain the fruition that marked Wotan's lifespan. Wotan nonetheless saw Siegfried as eternal because Wotan recognized in Siegfried the fundamental truth that the past and present must fade into the future. But even the most promising future must itself fade into the present and then become past, just as the young Siegfried, glowing with freedom and youthful power, quickly fades away in death. The "eternal" Siegfried's death epitomizes with special intensity the fact that the future is only as eternal as the next moment beyond the present. But this moment must exist, as the fading Wotan quickly discerns when in the presence of the young Siegfried, the heroic but ultimately and necessarily mortal embodiment of that moment.

In the confrontation between these two epochal and blood-related figures, the Wanderer struggles against part of himself while attempting to preserve his rule, just as in a much more literal sense he destroyed part of himself as a prerequisite to acquiring rule in the first place. This struggle between different aspects of the self is found not only in the blood line of the combatants but also in the symbolic composition of the weapons which they wield against one another. Wotan's spear was originally a branch from the world ash tree. Siegfried's sword has been reforged from the remnants of the sword originally in the possession of his father Siegmund. In the second act of *Die Walküre*, we learn that this sword was placed in a tree by Wotan when he attended the wedding of Sieglinde and Hunding, a Wotan hiding his divinity behind the same slouching hat he will wear later as the Wanderer. The stage directions at the end of act 1, scene 2 of *Die Walküre* designate the tree's species: it is an ash (*Eschenstamm*). Wotan thus saw to it that the natural receptacle for the sword accessible to Siegmund in time of great need was generically the same as the substance from which his own spear was drawn. When Siegmund's sword was eventually shattered, it was Wotan's spear by which the deed was accomplished. In this case, Wotan's own spear destroys the sword that Wotan himself had provided for the protection of his son and chosen hero.

When Wotan's grandson Siegfried resolves to forge the remnants of this sword, he makes the necessary fire from the charcoal of a tree. This tree is a "brown ash" (*Braune Esche*). According to Mime, Siegfried had been something less than an attentive pupil of Mime's craft, smithery. But Siegfried nonetheless manages to forge the sword with minimal effort and maximum speed. In Mime's words, the pupil teaches the teacher, at least in this instance. Therefore, some cause other than inspired technique contributed to an untutored smith's transmutation of shattered remains into a finished and world-fateful weapon. Could this cause be the special kind of fire leaping from the ash charcoal? If so, then the natural source of Wotan's power and the receptacle for Siegmund's sword are generically identical to the "stuff" by means of which Siegfried forges the sword that symbolically ends the power originally from the ash tree. In a sense, the power of the ash tree is destroyed by the fire of charcoal made from the ash tree (just as fire on a much larger scale will destroy the ash timbers piled at the base of Valhalla itself). Nature contains the seeds of its own self-purgation, at least that part of nature which has engendered the power to enforce the affairs of gods and men in this particular epoch.[6]

Within this domain of natural symbolism, other suggestive parallels may be drawn. For example, consider Wagner's skillful use of wood and water. It is in the natural order of things that a branch separated from its source of life must die. Thus, the construction of a wooden spear is the destruction of a living branch. The fact that Wotan's spear retained its resiliency and potency for as long as it did attests to the extensive quantity of power that the ash tree must have originally possessed. Wotan's regime, established as it was on the basis of power issuing from the institution of contracts, may have been finite, but its finitude was far from ephemeral. Furthermore, if this analogy is taken to its natural end, one may wonder whether the ash tree itself is, in its own way, as symbolically finite as its severed branch. For it is also in the natural order of things that all trees must die. The parallel between the finite nature of trees and the finitude of power symbolized by a broken tree branch suggests that power as such may have finite limits; the control and exercise of power may be necessarily finite simply because the natural source of that power is also necessarily finite.

For Wotan, the destruction of life in the form of a severed tree branch was required in order to construct a spear for the regulation of life on a higher order and grander scale. The same polar opposition between creation and destruction holds for water. Although trees are alive and water is not, water is essential for all life, regardless of what form that life may take. Nature's spring gave Wotan the wisdom to adopt the institution of contracts as a principle of order for all human and divine life. However, when the epoch of contracts had run its course, the Rhine would cleanse the world of a type of order that originated, at least symbolically, from a watery source of much smaller dimension. The raging waters of the Rhine become the source of a purgative disorder in direct contrast to the quiet waters of the spring, the source of an order that eventually grows polluted from abuse. Both as symbols and in fact, wood and water work for and against the highest forms of life, human and divine.

When Wotan the Wanderer exits from the world, he takes with him a tangible product of his past, the now splintered symbol of that prior wisdom and power which defined his limits as guardian of the world. When Siegfried goes on his way after the destruction of this spear, he, too, takes with him something tangible: that part of his blood line which he inherited from the now deposed Wotan. The extent of this relation may be attenuated, but it is present nonetheless. This presence will become more and more manifest after Siegfried learns fear by loving Brünnhilde and then testifies to this love by swearing oaths to that effect, oaths that are sanctioned by the institution of contracts, which now survives only by the weight of tradition. Wotan the Wanderer escaped the violation of contracts with his life, at least for a time. Siegfried will not have even this small comfort.

Siegfried and Brünnhilde

After Siegfried destroys the Wanderer's spear, the once-sacred contracts notched on that spear lose their fundamental binding authority. In fact, there is some reason to believe that the very institution of contracts itself has now been undermined, not merely the individual contracts supposedly guarded by Wotan. If the institution of contracts is a primary cause of the world's social harmony, then the destruction of that institution will disrupt, if not destroy, the harmony of the present world order. Wotan himself temporarily survives the destruction of his spear, and the institution of contracts survives in similar fashion. But Wotan is now only a figurehead ruler of no real substance. The contracts and oaths established from this point on will be likewise hollow in content, although formally embraced by the parties involved with serious intent to abide by their once obligatory conditions.

An interlocking series of such contractual events occurs from the end of the third act of *Siegfried* to the conclusion of the *Ring*. The first event involves Siegfried and Brünnhilde. Seigfried has won Brünnhilde by his boldness and by his passionate love, a love that, after some initial hesitation, Brünnhilde resolves to reciprocate. But passion is not the only bond that unites the two lovers. In the Prologue to *Götterdämmerung*, Brünnhilde tells Siegfried to "remember the oaths which make us one" (*Gedenk der Eide, / die uns einen*). Siegfried then takes the ring and gives it to Brünnhilde as a pledge of his commitment to his oath. Brünnhilde recognizes that commitment and does her best to honor it. Thus, when Waltraute implores Brünnhilde to return the ring to the Rhine where it belongs, Brünnhilde refuses, referring to the ring as Siegfried's "pledge of love" (*Liebespfand*). In turn, Siegfried receives from Brünnhilde the "holy runes" (*Heiliger Runen*) of divine wisdom that Brünnhilde had received from the gods and that she apparently retains even after her godhead has been stripped by Wotan at the conclusion of *Die Walküre*.

The oath of love between Siegfried and Brünnhilde, an oath sworn after the events of *Siegfried*, is attested to, both formally and substantively, by the contractual arrangements voiced in *Götterdämmerung*. Siegfried gives Brünnhilde the ring; Brünnhilde gives Siegfried the rudiments of divine wisdom. This visible exchange substantiates the purely verbal and formal swearing of the oath of love. As a result, Siegfried does not speak metaphorically when, in the third act of *Siegfried*, he refers to Brünnhilde as his "bride" (*Braut*) and as his "holy wife" (*heiliges Weib*). All the requisite conditions for the contract of matrimony have been met. Siegfried and Brünnhilde are no less husband and wife than Hunding and Sieglinde; the principal difference is that Siegfried and Brünnhilde are privately wedded to each other both by love and by mutual oaths, whereas Hunding and Sieglinde were publicly bound to each other only by a formal marital contract.

Unlike the typical modern matrimonial rite, the two lovers have, in this case, exchanged pledges qualitatively different from one another. The pledge given to Brünnhilde, a golden ring, is tangible; the pledge given to Siegfried, runic wisdom, is intangible. As far as the lovers are concerned, however, no discrepancy of any importance has marred the exchange; each lover believes that the pledge bestowed is no more or less valuable than the pledge received. But the ring, a golden artefact, is natural in a way that runic wisdom cannot be. As such, the ring may therefore be significant in the same way that Wotan's spear was significant. The earlier inquiry suggested that nature became unavoidably degenerate when transmuted from a living tree to a spear shaped from a branch of that tree. Of course, gold as a metal cannot degenerate in this way, since gold is by nature inanimate. But the power to transform the gold into a ring, especially this ring with its cosmic possibilities, came only as a result of a contractual exchange of fundamental importance. Thus, the true value of the ring may well reflect the true status of the institutional device by which that ring was formed. And if each pledge is, in fact, commensurate in value with its counterpart, then Brünnhilde's runic wisdom will be just as liable to degeneracy as Siegfried's golden ring. Since the ring shines with all the splendor naturally attendant to such an artifact, the lovers have no reason to suspect that such splendor conceals something that will eventually darken the entire world.

The mutual love of Siegfried and Brünnhilde is doubtless authentic. But, as the symbolic function of the ring has suggested, the oath and contractual pledges that each swore to the other may be something less than authentic. In fact, the cancerous condition of this oath will become evident once the respective pledges that seal its contractual nature are examined in some detail. With the benefit of hindsight, it will be seen that the substantiation of this oath is such that the lovers would have been far better off simply loving each other and not swearing an oath that they loved each other truly. By appealing to the institutional device of contracts—an institution now virtually devoid of effect—they set in motion a mutual belief in the reliability of this oath that, in conjunction with other circumstances, will eventually destroy the mortal existence of the two lovers, if not the transcendent quality of their love.

Brünnhilde pledges to Siegfried whatever wisdom she may possess by virtue of her "holy runes." The context suggests that these runes are emblematic of divine wisdom stamped according to the traditional outlines of Wotan's right of legitimacy. But recall that Brünnhilde's divinity has been stripped from her by Wotan at the end of *Die Walküre*—how then can she convey divine wisdom if she is no longer divine? Also, the light of divine wisdom has been effectively extinguished after the destruction of Wotan's spear—how then can divine wisdom be transferred if it is neither divine nor wisdom? In reply, first, Brünnhilde could still have retained vestiges of divine wisdom even though, according to the letter of Wotan's punishment, she was reduced from divine to mortal status. But second, and more important, although divine wisdom may be of finite duration, it nonetheless still lingers, just as Wotan's shadowy existence lingers in the silent halls of Valhalla. However, given the ultimately destructive effects such wisdom had on Wotan, Brünnhilde's subsequent conferral of the runes of that wisdom on Siegfried becomes a pledge of dubious value. If Wotan's wisdom finally fails him, can Siegfried be better served by what amounts to a mere shadow of that wisdom?

Brünnhilde's own testimony on her relation to wisdom reflects its presently uncertain status. When she faces the enraged Wotan in the third act of *Die Walküre*, she says to him that "I am not wise" (*Nicht weise bin ich*). In context, she may mean only that her wisdom is negligible in comparison with the paternal fountainhead of wisdom, not that her own measure of wisdom was nonexistent. However, at the conclusion of *Siegfried*, Brünnhilde confesses that whatever wisdom she once possessed has now vanished: "My wisdom is silent" (*Mein Wissen schweight*), she cries when Siegfried presses her to return his passion. And again, shortly thereafter, "heavenly wisdom rushes from me" (*himmlisches Wissen / stürmt mir dahin*), although this claim also suggests that she still retained some trace of wisdom, even though that wisdom may have sprung from a different source. In light of this possibility, consider her avowal shortly after Siegfried kisses her and they both experience love for the first time: "yet I am wise only because I love you" (*doch wissend bin ich / nur weil ich dich liebe*). Here Brünnhilde intimates that whatever wisdom she may possess results from love rather than, or perhaps in addition to, any vestiges of her divine lineage.

Brünnhilde thus recognizes the importance of wisdom, whether during a confrontation with her divine father, when she seems to have lost access to it, or in the company of her passionate lover, when she senses its presence but cannot pinpoint its origin. In both instances, Brünnhilde is placed before a male counterpart who represents the limits of the world with respect to a certain type of experience. With Wotan, that experience concerns authority; Brünnhlde learns that regardless of how powerful the reasons of the heart may be, authority must be honored and wisdom must be preserved, especially in order to determine the relative priority between the dictates of authority and the urgings of the heart when they conflict with one another. With Siegfried, that experience is love; here Brünnhilde becomes personally and intensely aware of that fundamental truth which she had witnessed only secondhand during her earlier conflict with Wotan: love must always be tempered with wisdom, even and especially in those instances when love is defined by great passion. Abashed and humbled before Wotan, ecstatic and overjoyed with Siegfried, the simple warrior Brünnhilde becomes progressively educated in the complex interaction between personal emotions and the impersonal forces that are essential for orderly and civilized life.

What then does Brünnhilde confer on Siegfried through the wisdom of her holy runes? No details are given in the poem, but in light of Siegfried's subsequent conduct with the Gibichungs, one may suppose that the runes bestowed by Brünnhilde are, at least in part, the same runes that were notched on Wotan's spear, i.e., the need to sanction serious proposals with contracts and oaths. Thus, regardless of whether Brünnhilde's wisdom is a reminiscence of her prior divinity or an extension of her present love, the letter of that wisdom is identical to the wisdom that guided the history of Wotan's regime. It is perhaps something more than mere happenstance that

Siegfried's tragically brief career parallels that of Wotan, for Siegfried, too, immediately becomes involved in a series of oaths that eventually lead to his demise, just as Wotan entered into contracts with the same result. If, for Siegfried, such must be the outcome of Brünnhilde's "holy runes," then Brünnhilde should have been less wise in her wisdom. The fact that Brünnhilde is unaware that the divine representative of wisdom survives only as a figurehead and the fact that she has given *all* that remains of her divine wisdom (*All mein Wissen*) jointly hasten the malignant spread of tragic consequences.

Siegfried's pledge to Brünnhilde contains similarly unintended duplicity. Siegfried gives her the golden ring, not for its intrinsic value, nor for its world-dominating potential (for he is ignorant of that potential), but as a symbol of the "virtue" (*Tugend*) in "whatever deeds" (*Taten je*) he has so far performed. As examples of virtuous deeds, Brünnhilde has already noted Siegfried's passage through the magic fire and his movement toward her sleeping form. To this list, Siegfried adds his slaying of the dragon Fafner. Although the forging of the sword Nothung, the execution of Mime, and the successful confrontation with the Wanderer are not cited, presumably some or all of these deeds are also virtuous in the sense Siegfried intends the bestowal of the ring to represent. The primary virtue present in each of these deeds is courage. But, in fact, Siegfried has performed all these deeds while *not knowing the meaning of fear.* He does not learn fear until he faces the sleeping Brünnhilde. How then can virtue, specifically the virtue of courage, be ascribed to certain putatively courageous acts when the performer of these acts was unaware that he had been involved in fearful situations, i.e., situations that required courage? To an individual who has never experienced the distinction between fear and courage, slaying a dragon is no more hazardous to self than brushing off a fly or a demonic dwarf; the slayer has no real appreciation for the situation he faces because he is impervious to the danger he supposedly braves. The same question may be raised concerning all the other deeds Siegfried attributes to virtue and to the ring as symbolic of that virtue.

Siegfried weds his past deeds to his present love so that Brünnhilde can have him, at least symbolically during his absence in quest of adventure, by possessing his pledged ring. But if virtue means something more than sheer rambunctious innocence, which must be the case if Siegfried is to manifest the heroic manliness required to win Brünnhilde, then the deeds that are aligned with virtue must be based on some cause other than a courage born from one who has never known fear. In a very real sense, the courage displayed by Siegfried is only external, only an appearance in the eyes of those who witness his deeds, and not internal to the man who performs those deeds. This is courage in name only and therefore not really courage at all, but a form of foolhardiness or perhaps even stupidity. Siegfried himself acknowledges his fundamental ignorance in this regard. When he is about to do battle with Fafner, the dragon asks him whether he has the arrogance to learn fear from one so horribly awe-inspiring. Siegfried replies:

> Mut oder Übermut,
> was weiss ich!
>
> (Courage or presumption,
> What do I know!)

I suggest that the flamboyant Siegfried's utterance should be taken quite literally in this context. Therefore, if the prospective hero does not in fact know the difference between the courage requisite for bravery and a bravado that is sheer braggadocio, then slaying a dragon in these circumstances hardly qualifies as a virtuous deed.

Although Siegfried eventually learns fear, he does so only during the process of satisfying his curiosity, a curiosity that swells into passion and then love for the now awakened Brünnhilde. But compare, in this context, Siegfried's fear of Brünnhilde with Wotan's fear of Alberich and the threat to Valhalla that Alberich represents. At the same time that Siegfried fears Brünnhilde, he finds himself mysteriously drawn to her precisely because his fear is mingled with curiosity. And, in fact, the fear vanishes altogether once the supposed object of fear begins to display a certain attitude of receptivity. On the other hand, Wotan's fear of Alberich is completely devoid of curiosity. Wotan is fully aware of what may happen to him, but in no sense of the term is Wotan curious about the precise nature of this dreaded although presently unexperienced reality. In both cases, fear is of the unknown. For Siegfried, the unknown may not be entirely unpleasant, hence the presence of fear mingled with curiosity. For Wotan, however, the unknown—dethronement and death—can only be worse than unpleasant, hence Wotan's abject horror of its realization and the distance he hopes to maintain between himself and all evil effects adhering to Alberich's cursed ring. To what degree is Siegfried's fear the kind of emotion that justifies calling his actions toward Brünnhilde courageous and thus virtuous? My own conviction is that Siegfried's fear pales, both in duration and in intensity, when compared to the fear Wotan must have undergone. But the point is that even if Siegfried's fear does in fact justify this one act as courageous, that act alone cannot substantiate Siegfried's oath of love to Brünnhilde. For this oath is clearly intended to include *all* those prior actions that, for Siegfried, result from virtue. However, as noted, in none of these actions did Siegfried have an experience of fear, a prime prerequisite for the manifestation of courage in the virtuous sense Siegfried intends.

Siegfried and Brünnhilde are lovers and they have exchanged pledges to sanction their love through the marital oath, just as Siegmund and Sieglinde did in *Die Walküre*. Surely neither intended to deceive the other in this oath (*Eid*). Unlike subsequent oaths in *Götterdämmerung* (which will be duly considered), their oath is meant to convey only the highest sentiments and to fulfill only the most noble obligations. But the fact remains that the substance of each pledge is not what the giver of that pledge believes it to be. Thus, the potential source of rupture in the apparently seamless progression from the onset of affection to the consummation of passionate love to the exchange of oaths as a sanction for that love lies not in love itself, nor in the intentions of the lovers, but in the institution that contractually binds the lovers to each other. If a serious misunderstanding occurs between Siegfried and Brünnhilde after their oath of love, this misunderstanding can only become more divisive once a misplaced trust in the reliability of the formal institution has sanctioned their love. The mutual trust in this oath is as powerful as the naked love that the oath has elevated to the level of social and moral righteousness. How could it be otherwise, given that the civilized world was established and remains to this very moment governed on the basis of such trust? But if well-intentioned trust is placed in an ineffectual and now malignant device, tragic consequences for the lovers in particular and for the world order in general can hardly be circumvented.

The love between Siegfried and Brünnhilde serves as the standard for determining the nature of love in the *Ring*, at least passionate love of rare intensity. The only relationship which can rival theirs in this respect is that between Siegmund and Sieglinde. However, the purity of this earlier instance of love is tainted by incest, adultery, and bigamy. None of these immoral features affects the love between Siegfried and Brünnhilde. In addition, both lovers are more intimately related to the race of the divinities, the highest form of consciousness in the *Ring*: Siegfried—a hero hand-picked by the king of the gods; Brünnhilde—a heroic warrior who, for a time, actually shared in divine consciousness. Siegmund's love for Sieglinde is passionate, to be sure, but the degree of its passion is surely less intense than Siegfried's tempestuous love for Brünnhilde. (One might appeal to the difference between the finale to act 1 of *Die Walküre* and the finale to act 3 of *Siegfried* for purely musical substantiation of this contention.) Nevertheless, however intense and pure that passion might be, the love between Siegfried and Brünnhilde remains connected to an oath, a type of contract. Although love and oaths need never have anything to do with one another—since one can love deeply without swearing an oath to that effect and one can swear an oath without loving the individual to whom the oath is sworn, the fact that the most exalted expression of love in the *Ring* becomes subject to an oath will make it difficult for love even of this intensity to survive.

Siegfried, Gunther, and Hagen

At the conclusion of the Prologue to *Götterdämmerung*, Siegfried leaves Brünnhilde in search of adventure, just as Wotan had left Fricka in order to fulfill his divine nature by pursuing the blandishments hidden in such variety and change. Siegfried lands on the shores of the Gibichungs, greets the Gibichung leader Gunther, and initiates their acquaintance by challenging him either to fight or be friends. Gunther elects friendship and seals his bond with an oath—"may my life make good my oath" (*Eide*). Siegfried reciprocates this oath—"may my sword make good my oath" (*Eide*). Thus, Siegfried continues the contractual tradition by substantiating his oath with his sword in a manner analogous to the way Wotan had substantiated *all* oaths with his spear. But of course Siegfried's sword has destroyed Wotan's spear, thereby disestablishing the institution represented by that spear. Although Siegfried's thoughts are unknown at this point, his actions toward Gunther indicate a conviction that the authority once invested in that spear has somehow been transferred to his sword in virtue of the destruction of the spear by that sword. The extent to which that institution retains its prior efficacy is now marginal at best. Yet even as the two men swear this oath, the contract leitmotif is again heard in the orchestra—the tradition of contracts and oaths persists externally in both word and music, if not in substance.

To celebrate his new friendship, Siegfried drinks from a horn containing a magic potion. This potion eventually induces him to act in accordance with the long-range interest of three accomplices—Gunther, his sister Gutrune, and Alberich's son Hagen, the plot's chief perpetrator. The potion begins to take effect almost immediately; Siegfried loses all recollection of Brünnhilde and becomes enamored of Gutrune. He also learns that Gunther desires to wed Brünnhilde. At this point, Siegfried and Gunther swear yet another oath, this time to their mutual "blood brotherhood" (*Blutbrüderschaft*) and to the fulfillment of their respective desires. Since blood brotherhood is a much more intimate relation than friendship, one may presume that all obligations incumbent from the first oath have become subsumed under the obligations arising from the second oath. To seal the second oath more securely, Siegfried and Gunther prick their arms and bleed into the drinking horn; both men then partake of the libation. Hagen holds the horn, but refuses to take part in the oath because, as he puts it, his own blood is "stubborn and cold" (*störrisch und kalt*) and therefore prevents his participation in such a "fiery bond" (*feurigen Bund*). Later, however, Hagen will shrug off his sham reticence and become more than actively involved in this particular contractual commitment.

Siegfried and Gunther have mingled their blood, an especially intimate form of consanguinity. But they have also radically increased the degree of intimacy by actually imbibing the vital liquid. When Wotan drank from the spring of nature's wisdom, he learned that the institution of contracts was a prerequisite for authority and power. Now, as Wotan's epoch in world history comes to a close, his grandson also drinks to acknowledge the fundamental character of the oath as a contractually binding commitment. The fact that the liquid Siegfried drinks is his own blood rather than nature's water shows the seriousness with which this particular oath has been taken. However, the substitution of human blood for natural water symbolizes that this oath will be only as effective as Siegfried's own experience and character. Thus, if Siegfried lacks experience or depth of character, the very intimacy of this blood-oath becomes an ironic commentary on the true status of the oath. Siegfried has attested to the oath by an act of self-mutilation in which the agent sheds his own blood, but this blood, from a mortal source with distinctively mortal inadequacies, is at best a pale reflection of the natural vitality present in the original spring water by means of which the very act of swearing an oath was first legitimatized. The coldness of Hagen's blood is a direct counterpart to the heat of youthful exuberance and adventurousness in the blood of Siegfried. Hagen has thus separated himself from Siegfried's oath by appealing to a fundamental difference in temperament between them. But this distance has a deeper significance, for the very coldness of Hagen's blood points to the lack of life in the institutional status of the oath to which the hot-blooded Siegfried has just sworn and the icy Hagen has sanctioned.

Siegfried has supplanted his oath of fidelity to Brünnhilde with two additional oaths, both contracted with Gunther. The first oath between the two men is at least formally authentic, since each knows what he is doing when he swears the oath and why he is doing it. But, regardless of its formal correctness, this oath cannot be authentic and binding in the traditional manner if, as suggested above, that very tradition has been uprooted. And, in fact, the empty formalism of Siegfried's first oath to Gunther is indirectly symbolized by the conditions which surround the second oath. For this oath has been sworn to only *after* Siegfried has partaken of the potion. As a result of the potion's magic, Siegfried has forgotten that he had sworn an oath of fidelity to Brünnhilde. But given these conditions, one may wonder how Siegfried can be held responsible for his subsequent promise to Gunther and his actions in support of that promise. Why does Siegfried, now reduced to little more than a heroic puppet by a deceptive and magically induced oath, suffer the tragic fate that will be his to suffer? The answer to this difficult question will be important as far as determining the extent to which the decay of the institution of contracts affects characters other than Wotan, especially the heroic Siegfried.

To prepare the way for the answer that I shall propose, let me first examine the effect of Siegfried's oath to Brünnhilde as conjoined with his second oath to Gunther. We discern that, in fact, the two oaths directly conflict with one another. If Siegfried fulfills his oath to Brünnhilde, he breaks his oath to Gunther (since by his oath of blood brotherhood he had vowed to bring Brünnhilde back as Gunther's prospective bride); if he fulfills his oath to Gunther, then he breaks his oath to Brünnhilde (since the oath sanctioning their married love implies a monogamous state for both parties). Siegfried must choose one of these two alternatives. He does not have the option of, for example, simply leaving the land of the Gibichungs in search of other adventures, for his departure in these circumstances would, in effect, break his oath to Gunther to secure Brünnhilde as Gunther's bride. Therefore, it is important to be aware of the fact that the course of events dictated by the conjunction of Siegfried's oath to Brünnhilde and his second oath to Gunther requires that one of these two oaths *must* be broken. The formal authenticity of Siegfried's second oath may be suspect, as suggested above. Nevertheless, Siegfried believes that this oath is binding; as a result, in his own mind he is no less obligated by that oath, regardless of what its real status may be.

Siegfried's oath to Brünnhilde was engendered by love, while his second oath to Gunther was incited by a magical potion. Had he not become involved in this second oath, Siegfried would never have been locked into a situation that was both irreversible and inextricable. The point that should be made at this stage concerns the connection between the unnatural origin of this second oath and what may well turn out to be the unnatural quality of the institution of contracts itself. In other words, I suggest (and will argue the matter later) that the significance of the second oath be determined in conjunction with the fact that this oath was induced by magic, i.e., by an essentially non-natural means. Viewed from this perspective, the second oath becomes emblematic of the true nature of the institution that, perhaps necessarily, evolved in such a way that a heroic mortal, availing himself of that institution from apparently the most noble motives, became entrapped and ultimately doomed by that very institution.

Siegfried decides to fulfill his oath to Gunther. Disguised by the Tarnhelm to resemble Gunther, he forces Brünnhilde to give him the ring pledged to her by Siegfried. He rips the ring from her finger. Notice the parallel between this robbery, as Brünnhilde perceives it (*du Räuber!*), and Wotan's theft of the ring from Alberich. Alberich had contracted for the ring by foreswearing love; Brünnhilde had sealed her oath of love by contractually exchanging her holy runes of wisdom for the virtue supposedly represented by Siegfried's ring. But whereas Wotan stole the ring and knowingly violated Alberich's contract, Siegfried stole the ring completely unaware of violating Brünnhilde's contractual oath. And Siegfried, or rather the man Siegfried became after taking the potion and wearing the Tarnhelm, is now breaking his original oath to her in the process of satisfying a subsequent oath he made to Gunther.

The following day, Brünnhilde is brought by Gunther into the ceremonial hall of the Gibichungs. There she sees Siegfried, still under the sway of the potion and still ignorant of her as his beloved. Brünnhilde, noticing that Siegfried has the ring which had been wrested from her by Gunther, asks Gunther to take back the "pledge" (*Pfand*) from Siegfried. Although the ring was acquired through force, Brünnhilde appears resigned to the fact that ownership of the ring is tantamount to marital legitimacy: whoever owns the ring may lay claim to be her legal husband. Gutrune asks Siegfried whether Brünnhilde was "wedded" (*vermählte*) to him during the previous evening, and Siegfried assents, although the disguised Siegfried only stood proxy until she could be married to Gunther according to the demands of Gibichung protocol. Thus, her present concern to have the ring returned from Siegfried (who, disguised as Gunther, was the real thief) to Gunther (who Brünnhilde had thought was the real thief by virtue of the disguise) maintains the strict obligation of Brünnhilde's marital oath, even when it has become applicable to someone for whom she has neither love nor affection.

Siegfried is now enmeshed within precisely the precarious situation which Hagen had planned. The cunning Hagen proclaims, and none too subtly (perhaps for the benefit of the vassals in attendance), that Siegfried acquired the ring through "fraud" (*Trug*) and that he should therefore make amends for his misdeed. Siegfried's honor is at stake, and he responds by swearing yet another oath. Significantly, Hagen offers the point of his spear as a locus of legitimacy for this oath. Siegfried swears an "eternal oath" (*ewigen Eide*) on the point of Hagen's spear that he did not break the oath (*Eide*) with his blood brother Gunther. For Siegfried, this oath publicizes the purity and nobility of his actions during and after the procurement of Brünnhilde for Gunther. In response, Brünnhilde, too, swears an "eternal oath" (*ewigen Eide*), also on Hagen's spear point, that Siegfried has broken all his prior oaths; in fact, she insists that he has committed "perjury" (*Meineid*) by swearing just now that he did not break these oaths.[7]

This final and indeed epochal set of oaths gathers together love, honor, and obligation in a tense and unstable unity. Siegfried and Brünnhilde love each other, but on the one hand Siegfried has forgotten his love and on the other hand Brünnhilde, with considerable justification, believes that her love is no longer reciprocated. Siegfried must protect his honor as a hero of virtue, especially now that he is in the presence of both the Gibichung royalty and its vassalage. Brünnhilde must protect her honor as a woman who remained faithful to her spouse, the absence of love for that spouse notwithstanding. And since both Siegfried and Brünnhilde have previously sworn oaths, these final oaths also evoke their awareness that they must stand by their obligation to these prior oaths, even if that obligation necessitates the swearing of still another oath. From the standpoint of oaths and the institution of contracts from which they originate, this is perhaps the climactic episode of the entire *Ring*. Wotan, alone and desolate while waiting for the end in the inner reaches of Valhalla, now exercises only a perfunctory and figurehead influence—the dramatic center has shifted earthward, to a would-be hero and a warrior woman who was once of divine lineage. The intensity of their love has magnified these two characters to the point where, if the world has any hope of salvation or redemption, it must be accomplished through their presence and agency. But the love that was once so prominent now exists and does not exist, an eerie indeterminate state which will become stable only when the obligations attendant upon their respective oaths are honorably resolved. The most exalted of passionate loves waits on the resolution of one apparently simple oath.

Wagner's stage directions for this crucial episode are subtle and revealing. The male vassals who have been witnessing the tense confrontation "close into a ring" (*schliessen einen Ring*) around Siegfried and Hagen before Siegfried swears his renunciatory oath. When Siegfried is finished, Brünnhilde "steps raging into the ring" (*tritt wütend in den Ring*). Thus, the oathtakers are surrounded by mortal men of low social order who react to what they see by forming, almost as if by instinct, a figure that precisely duplicates in shape the golden ring over which the present controversy rages. The concentric circles of humanity and power provide a new dimension to the institution of contracts. The oaths linking Siegmund to Sieglinde and Siegfried to Brünnhilde were exchanged in private. Only those who swore them knew of their existence. Now, however, the oaths by Siegfried and Brünnhilde are public, in full view of both the highest social class and the lowest vassals. It is true that in *Das Rheingold* a mixed audience was present when Wotan reneged on his contract, but in that instance gods and giants were the only active participants—not humans. Also, both parties were personally involved in that contract. In this case, however, the vassals ringing the series of oaths are little more than interested observers. But their witness is important nonetheless, both because of the democratic dimension cited above and because public support for the legitimacy of the oaths will become instrumental in the successful completion of Hagen's conspiracy.

Siegfried convinces Gunther that Brünnhilde's wrath will quickly dissipate, and he leaves with his affianced Gutrune to join in the wedding festivities. After witnessing what appears to be his cavalier and even sacrilegious conduct, Brünnhilde is readily persuaded by Hagen to seek vengeance against Siegfried. In concert with Gunther, the trio plan the circumstances that will culminate in Siegfried's death. Brünnhilde and Gunther call on Wotan, the "guardian of oaths" (*Eideshort*), to heed and sanction their plan of revenge. Brünnhilde shares in this appeal to tradition even though she has learned from Waltraute of Wotan's helpless resignation to his fate. In any case, and with or without Wotan's guardianship, Hagen accomplishes their joint desire by slaying Siegfried with a blow from his spear, the same spear on which Siegfried had sworn his final oath. Hagen justifies this consummate deed by exclaiming, "I have avenged perjury!" (*Meineid rächt' ich!*). He then quickly departs.

Wotan's authority and power have been effectively nullified by Siegfried; nevertheless, Wotan as guardian of oaths is explicitly invoked by Brünnhilde and Gunther to provide the ultimate sanction for vengeance on Siegfried's putative violation of his oaths. The institutional aspect of the oath as a type of contract still survives as a tradition, even though the source and substance of that tradition borders on extinction. The tradition remains tangibly evident in the figure of Hagen, the half-man, half-dwarf, groomed by his father Alberich as the polar opposite to Wotan in character but as Wotan's proposed replacement as guardian of the world. Hagen's spear sanctions the oath sworn to by Siegfried against Brünnhilde's sworn contention of dishonesty, an oath asserting that all his previous oaths were contractually sound and honored as such. Thus, Hagen's spear safeguards the only oath Siegfried swore after he had destroyed Wotan the Wanderer's spear.

Before his demise, Wotan was responsible for sanctioning and enforcing all oaths and contracts with his spear. But in a turn of events both ironic and poignant, Hagen now performs precisely the same function. The function of the spear remains constant, even though the source of power behind that function has shifted from the divine to the demonic. In view of this stark polar contrast in sanctioning authority, the fact that both Siegfried and Brünnhilde designated their oaths as "eternal" merely heightens the irony. Do they mean that the very process of swearing an oath is eternally reliable or that what they are swearing to in this particular oath is eternally true? Neither alternative proves to be the case: Wotan and all that he represents is on the verge of doom, while Siegfried swears to the equivalent of a lie, and Brünnhilde swears to a truth that was generated by false and unnatural deception. Although an oath as a contractual device may have appeared at some point in this epoch to be defined by eternity, this distinctive mode of temporality no longer applies to that device. When Siegfried and Brünnhilde both appeal to the eternal at a moment when the very nature of an oath is, in all respects, anything but eternal, they call attention to this nature, both its past and its future. The history of its origin and development has already been seen; what, one may wonder, will be its future?

The point of Hagen's spear replaces, although only temporarily, the shaft of Wotan's spear. But Hagen no less than Wotan still stands under the need to direct his most important actions by the obligational aspect of the institution of contracts. The second act of *Götterdämmerung* opens with one of the most striking scenes in the entire *Ring*, the brief but powerful meeting between Alberich and his son Hagen. The shadowy Alberich looms into Hagen's dreamy consciousness and urges his carefully tutored offspring to persist in the attempt to reacquire the ring for their mutual benefit. With the ring, father and son will together "inherit the world" (*erben die Welt*). Alberich asks, "Will you swear it?" (*Schwörst du mir's*), and Hagen consents to swear to obtain the ring. But notice that Hagen does not swear this intent to Alberich—rather, he swears it to himself (*Mir selbst schwör' ich's*). On the surface, this self-directed oath suggests that Hagen may not be particularly anxious to share the world with his father, if and when he should procure the ring. Thus, Hagen swears an oath to himself while in Alberich's presence merely to reconfirm the extent of his own passion for attaining the ring, not to provide a guarantee of sorts to Alberich that he will seriously pursue the ring as an accomplice in Alberich's grand scheme. But the deeper significance, I suggest, concerns the fact that Hagen has acceded to a tradition to which his father Alberich had appealed—somewhat ironically, given that Alberich originally lost the ring by virtue of a violation of that very tradition, but has invoked this tradition in a way that indicates that its real efficacy begins and ends in one individual. Hagen has become a law unto himself, at least with respect to the ultimate source of legitimacy for the oath he now swears. However, can an institution be authorized in this way? Surely not. Note, therefore, that Hagen's sleepiness in swearing this oath to himself mirrors the sleepiness of Erda's earthly wisdom when she last appears in *Siegfried*. In each case, the character's real substance has all but vanished, and in each case, this loss is manifested in the dream-like, almost surrealistic state of the protagonists involved. Nevertheless, even when the twilight of the gods and the purgation of the world have become imminent, the lowest and the highest form of consciousness remain bound by the convention of oaths.

I suggested earlier that Alberich had at least as much right to the ring as anyone, and perhaps more, given the nature of his original contractual exchange that allowed the ring to be created. Therefore, one could perhaps maintain that Hagen, having succeeded Alberich, could simply claim the ring by right of succession. But Hagen slays the heroic Siegfried in order to obtain the ring. Furthermore, Hagen does not justify his act with the above argument, but with the assertion that he has avenged perjury. Thus, one must evaluate Hagen's right to the ring in light of what he actually said rather than in light of what he might have said.

If Siegfried's final oath—the oath sworn to on the point of Hagen's spear—was, in fact, an instance of perjury, then Hagen would have the right to avenge this violated oath by taking the life of the perjuror, just as Wotan allowed the weaker Hunding to slay the stronger Siegmund in order to avenge Siegmund's violation of the oath Hunding swore when he wed Sieglinde. But the two cases may not be parallel in every essential sense—Siegmund was, after all, certainly guilty of adultery; but was Siegfried just as guilty of perjury? One must examine the situation and see where reason leads. Perjury is lying under oath. One must know the truth in order to lie. Because he had partaken of the magic potion administered by Hagen,

Siegfried no longer knew the truth, that he had previously sworn an oath of fidelity to Brünnhilde. Therefore, Siegfried could not have lied, since his state of mind precluded the very possibility of lying, at least concerning that particular action. And if he did not lie under oath, then of course he did not perjure himself. Should this reasoning be sound, then Hagen dissimulates when his execution of Siegfried is justified by the claim that he has "avenged perjury."

Deciding whether or not Siegfried was guilty of perjury becomes crucial for determining the legitimacy of Hagen's claim to rightful possession of the ring. Judged solely by the testimony of two of the principal characters, the issue remains in doubt. Thus, the weak and vacillating Gunther wonders aloud, "Did he break the bond?" and "Did he betray me?" Furthermore, Gunther knew that Siegfried had been married to Brünnhilde and thus must have known that such perjurous conduct was hardly likely from a man of heroic proportion. However, when Brünnhilde learns of the true circumstances surrounding Siegfried's death, she cries that "no one swore oaths more genuinely than he" (*Echter als er / schwur keiner Eide*); she then immediately adds that "none like him betrayed (*trog*) all oaths, all contracts." Gunther may waver in pronouncing judgment, but the bereaved Brünnhilde does not; the oaths Siegfried swore were authentic, and she is convinced that he broke those oaths. In fact, his actions were doubly false; Siegfried not only desired to wed Gutrune (when he had previously sworn fidelity to Brünnhilde) but he also forced Brünnhilde to become Gunther's bride (thus compelling her to violate her own oath to Siegfried). For Brünnhilde, these actions are immoral in the most virulent sense.

But in addition to the positions held by Gunther and Brünnhilde, yet another verdict—from an important and perhaps even unimpeachable source—is rendered on Siegfried's conduct. After Siegfried refuses to return the ring to their safekeeping, the three Rhinemaidens begin swimming about in an agitated manner. They then chorus in unison that although Siegfried deems himself wise and strong, his actions of late have belied his high self-estimation. For

> Eide schwur er—
> und achtet sie nicht;
>
> (he swore oaths—
> and he does not respect them;)

According to Brünnhilde, Siegfried has betrayed "all" oaths. The Rhinemaidens are less inclusive in their accusation, but perhaps more accurate, for they claim only that Siegfried does not respect "oaths," i.e., more than one. To which oaths do the Rhinemaidens refer? The first oath must be that sworn to Brünnhilde, which Siegfried does not respect when he weds Gutrune. However, there must be another violated oath in order to vindicate the accuracy of the Rhinemaidens' judgment. Upon examination, only the oath Siegfried swore on Hagen's spear-point can be construed as an oath that Siegfried did not respect. But this conclusion depends on the truth of the assumption that the oath to Gunther sworn under the influence of the potion is, in fact, a legitimate oath. For, as argued above, that oath must be legitimate if Siegfried's subsequent and final oath of truthfulness is, as Hagen claims, to become perjured.

The testimony of the Rhinemaidens is important, not merely because it agrees in substance with that of Brünnhilde, but for two additional reasons. First, unlike Brünnhilde, the Rhinemaidens have not been personally wounded by Siegfried's conduct. Their sole concern is to secure the return of the ring, not to redress wrongs done to them by virtue of any oaths, devious or otherwise. Second, as beings who naturally dwell in the water, the Rhinemaidens are closer to nature itself than Brünnhilde or Gunther or any other potential human judge of Siegfried. Thus, perhaps their sentiments approximate the verdict that nature—the ultimate source for the legitimacy of all contracts and oaths—would render on Siegfried's conduct. The sudden and abrupt transformation in the Rhinemaidens' character should be noted in this context. They are as serious now with Siegfried as they were frivolous just a few moments before. One suspects that the Rhinemaidens have ceased to be flighty fishy females and have become an anthropomorphic trio speaking the judgment of nature itself. Thus, the more the Rhinemaidens are identified as a personification of nature, the more weight one must grant to the verdict that Siegfried is indeed guilty of violating at least some and perhaps all of the oaths he swore.

But the moral judgment shared by Brünnhilde and the Rhinemaidens ignores what is surely the exculpatory fact of the magic potion. For it seems clear that had Siegfried not drunk this potion, he would not have broken his oath to Brünnhilde and thus would never have been in a position in which perjury could have arisen. If the verdict on Siegfried's final oath is based on Brünnhilde's testimony, as seconded by the Rhinemaidens, then Siegfried did in fact commit perjury. Brünnhilde voices this testimony in the great climactic monologue of the *Ring*, and there is no reason to think that she spends her last few earthly moments wallowing in self-pity and self-delusion. Her condemnation of Siegfried cannot be ignored as so much vented spleen. On the contrary, it is precisely because Siegfried had loved her and yet at the same time had sworn falsely about this love that Brünnhilde found it essential to initiate the final destruction of a regime that was founded on the reliability of oaths and contracts. The full complement of Brünnhilde's reasons for igniting the Valhalla holocaust are complex and will be examined in the next and concluding section of chapter 2. For now, it is sufficient to note the fact that Brünnhilde considered Siegfried guilty and to interpret that fact.

The correctness of Brünnhilde's moral judgment implies that the magic potion that induced Siegfried to commit perjury was not, in fact, an exculpatory factor after all. It then becomes essential to interpret the significance of the magical potion in relation to the oaths that it affects. From this perspective, I suggest that one should not view the potion (as, for instance, Shaw did) merely as a fillip to remind Wagner's audience that dramatic devices often found in "grand" opera could also serve the more grandiose aims of music dramas. The potions that induce Siegfried to swear the oath of blood brotherhood and later to regain his memory of Brünnhilde (when it is expedient for Hagen that the truth be revealed publicly) are essentially magical. And, as noted above, magic of this sort runs contrary to the normal flux of natural processes. The artificial and indeed unnatural quality of the magical substance provides a key to discovering a more penetrating reason for its presence in this context. For if the unnatural quality of these potions is seen in conjunction with the present state of the institution of contracts and oaths, then the hollow artificiality of the latter is summarized symbolically by the artificiality of the magic that has led instrumentally to the destruction of Siegfried, Brünnhilde, and the entire Valhallan regime.

I have already discussed how Siegfried's oath of fidelity necessarily conflicts with his oath of blood brotherhood to Gunther. The nature of this conflict is such that it points to a decisive feature in the very structure of the institution of contracts and oaths. When two oaths are so related that the fulfillment of the one necessitates the negation of the other, the artificial and ultimately self-destructive character of the institution becomes manifest. Thus, perhaps contracts are intrinsically restrictive, perhaps they inevitably hamper and distort the growth and development of life. The magic of the potion that instigates this internal conflict merely epitomizes the ultimately "unnatural" character of that institution. The potion then becomes a signal pointing to the ultimately unnatural quality of all oaths and all contracts and does not serve merely as a causal factor in one isolated instance of a fatal conspiracy based on an artificially elicited oath. Although that institution is traceable to natural sources, the history of the institution may be only of finite duration with respect to nature's infinitely diversified forms of life.[8]

This interpretation, which connects the potion with the institution of contracts, suggests an especially intimate relation between the manifest artificiality of the potion and the latent artificiality of contracts and oaths. As far as the potion itself is concerned, the relation need not be pursued. But if this symbolic connection between the potion and oaths is relevant, it becomes crucial to determine whether the *Ring* conveys the notion that the institution of contracts is somehow an intrinsically corrupt form for the establishment of the order necessary to civilization. The import of a problem of this magnitude transcends the personal concerns of the individuals involved. The presence and actions of the vassals indicate that the proper handling of oaths cuts across all social and class distinctions. It is the vassals who insist that Siegfried swear the oath (*schwöre den Eid!*) on Hagen's spear to rebut Brünnhilde's charge. And Hagen appeals directly to them to judge his right to claim the ring for himself after Siegfried's death (*richtet mein Recht!*). The universal social impact of oaths and contracts, always implicit in the *Ring*, becomes dramatically explicit toward the end of *Götterdämmerung*. Whether or not the poem of the *Ring* reaches a definitive conclusion on the status of this type of social bond will be a principal theme of the epilogue to this study.

I have given reasons to support the truth of Brünnhilde's moral assessment of the oaths sworn to by Siegfried. But if Brünnhilde was correct, Siegfried was in some essential respect guilty of perjury. And one then seems compelled to accept the legitimacy of Hagen's claim to have avenged perjury by slaying Siegfried. Furthermore, Hagen can also assert his right to the ring, since he descends directly from Alberich, the ring's original rightful owner, and since he has won at least the tacit consent of the vassals to the fact of his ownership. Now earlier the parallel between Hagen and Wotan with respect to their positions as guardian of oaths was noted. Wotan, too, sought the ring, but forfeited his right to it because he violated a series of contracts. The parallel between Wotan and Hagen suggests that Hagen will also forfeit his right to the ring if his actions have been similar to Wotan's in this respect. And, in fact, Hagen is no less guilty than Wotan. Hagen's use of oaths in pursuit of the ring has been as devious as Alberich's original loss of the ring was foolish; his machinations while supposedly guarding oaths are as cold-blooded and calculating as Wotan's were hot-blooded and impetuous.

When Wotan witnessed the passionate love between Siegmund and Sieglinde, he felt justified in abrogating, at least temporarily, the marital oath against which the lovers had sinned. Although Wotan eventually inflicted mortal punishment on Siegmund, he did so only under severe pressure from Fricka. But Hagen, who has succeeded Wotan as the guardian of oaths, is completely insensitive to the love between Siegfried and Brünnhilde, a love that doubtless exceeds that of Siegmund and Sieglinde in both intensity and nobility. For Hagen, naked power has replaced all dimensions of love, whether carnal or spiritual. In fact, Hagen is not only immune to the pleasures of love, but he actively arranges a set of circumstances that will insure the destruction of that love which binds Siegfried and Brünnhilde so intimately to one another. Hagen has concocted the potion that will place Siegfried in a position such that he cannot avoid perjuring himself; and he has induced Brünnhilde to seek Siegfried's death as vengeance for the supposed wrong he has done her, a particular deviltry that excites Gutrune to the point of cursing Hagen (*Verfluchter Hagen!*) when she finally realizes what has happened. Furthermore, Hagen's avowed protection of the oath sworn to on his spear-point is as much a sham as the oath itself. For he fully intends to slay Siegfried at the first opportune moment, a moment that is inevitable, given the treacherous substance of the oath. Hagen treats oaths no less shamefully than Wotan treated contracts, but for different motives. Whereas Wotan violated contracts in order to maintain and increase power he already possessed, Hagen violated oaths in order to acquire power that, as far as he was concerned, belonged rightfully to him and to his wronged father Alberich. Hagen may have "avenged perjury," but his execution of Siegfried can be so categorized only in the most abstract sense. Given the pre-eminence of the contractual dimension, both Hagen and Wotan have fallen prey to their own weakness by way of abusing the very institution that presented the opportunity to realize their dreams of almighty power.

Finally, the details of Wagner's staging are again crucial in visually evoking the symbolic importance of Hagen's relation to oaths and contracts. The *shaft* of Wotan's spear contains the records of binding contracts and, as such, represents the only legitimate source of authority bestowed by nature. The point of the spear is both a symbol and a practical instrument of the power based on that authority. But when Hagen's surrogate spear authorizes an oath, only the appearance of legitimate authority remains. Wagner carefully indicates this by having both Siegfried and Brünnhilde swear their oaths on the *point* of Hagen's spear rather than on its shaft. Although Hagen's spear possesses the instrumental power that any spear would possess, that power lacks proper legitimacy, given that the source of this legitimacy has been effectively blocked off once the shaft of Wotan's spear was shattered by Siegfried.

Brünnhilde: Love and the Oaths of Love

Despite all the apparent heroics of a Siegfried, it is a woman who performs the requisite "world redeeming" act. Brünnhilde's principal reasons for igniting the climactic fire that destroys the remnants of a defunct world order emerge from the confrontation between her love for Siegfried and her trust in the oaths that sanctioned their love. My analysis of the function of contracts will conclude by examining this confrontation.

The Brünnhilde who was wooed, wed, and wronged by Siegfried is not the Brünnhilde who first appears in act 2 of *Die Walküre*. There she is a warrior goddess, the favorite daughter of Wotan, his confidante and, in a sense, his alter ego. However, Brünnhilde forfeits this high station when she disobeys Wotan's command to permit Siegmund's death; as punishment, Wotan strips her godhead and reduces her to the level of other mortal women. But although Brünnhilde has broken the "holy bond" (*seligen Bund*) with Wotan, she refuses to believe that she can be entirely displaced from her nature as a divinity. Brünnhilde exhorts Wotan that surely he cannot dishonor "what is an eternal part of you" (*Dein ewig Teil*). Thus, Brünnhilde sees herself remaining at least to some degree divine even after Wotan surrounds her with the magic fire. And with divinity surely comes eternity. For Wotan, the future dictates that time itself will become finite after his first and final meeting with Siegfried. But at this point, neither Wotan nor, of course, Brünnhilde have any reason to believe that eternity will not be part of the gods' nature. And it is important, I suggest, to determine Brünnhilde's nature after Wotan has taken away her divinity. For if she is still in some sense eternal, her subsequent assertions concerning contracts, oaths, and love will carry more significance than if she were merely "mortal." Brünnhilde would remain in contact with those "timeless" elements which grounded and animated the world until the destruction of the regime established on the basis of those elements. And her language would reflect her awareness of this eternal realm to the extent that she still participated in that realm.

Two passages in the third act of *Siegfried* indicate that Brünnhilde was aware of considerably more than someone of non-divine station could possibly have known. In the midst of her passionate avowals of love for Siegfried, Brünnhilde reveals that she had loved him even *before he was conceived* (*noch eh du gezeugt*). Thus, Brünnhilde must have been aware by some sort of sympathetic feeling of the "thought" (*Gedanke*) hidden deep in Wotan's consciousness, the thought of creating the conditions whereby a hero could, of his own accord, redeem the gods with honor. Since Wotan thinks this thought from love of himself as a divinity, Brünnhilde can also love the thought of the hero (Siegfried) before that hero has been conceived in the physical sense. But this prior "felt" unity with Seigfried is possible only on condition that she retains an almost metaphysical affinity with her eternal father, especially with his wishes and desires. Since her awareness of this affinity remains *after* Wotan's divestiture of her divinity, Brünnhilde must retain some semblance of the divinity she possessed when the feeling of affinity first occurred.

The second passage is found shortly thereafter. At the very peak of her amorous ecstasy, Brünnhilde calls on the Norns to "rend" (*Zerreisst*) the ropes that bind their epochal runes. But how could she know that the ropes of runic wisdom woven by the Norns *should* be broken (as, in fact, they will be broken in the first scene of *Götterdämmerung*) unless she was in some respect prescient? Brünnhilde's vision of the future is similar both in accuracy and in content to Sieglinde's prophetic awareness as manifested toward the end of act 2 of *Die Walküre*. Just before Siegmund meets Brünnhilde, Sieglinde deliriously reports witnessing the splintering of Siegmund's sword and the toppling of the ash tree, presumably the world ash tree. Sieglinde's vision is born from delirium (it is "*wahnsinnig*," according to

Wagner's staging), while Brünnhilde's is born from love. However, the fact that Brünnhilde possesses awareness of the future implies that in this respect she was at least as eternal as that fate which the Norns administered.

These two passages show that Brünnhilde remains partially in contact with that aspect of eternity still present in her divine father and in the Norns. She may no longer be able to perform all the functions of a warrior goddess, but in terms of remembering her own divine past and in her capacity for prescient knowledge Brünnhilde retains a significant portion of her former nature. For this reason, her final stated position on the relation between love and the oaths that sanction love will be all the more crucial.

Brünnhilde has already forcefully indicated the highest regard for Siegfried's love and for the oath that sealed this love. In the first act of *Götterdämmerung,* her warrior sister Waltraute hurriedly arrives from Valhalla, reports on the passive condition of Wotan and his collection of heroes, and implores Brünnhilde to return the ring to the depths of the Rhine. The "world's troubles" (*Der Welt Unheil*) spring from the ring; only if it is returned to the Rhinemaidens will both the race of gods and the world be purged of its evil. But Brünnhilde is shocked at Waltraute's request—"*Siegfrieds Liebespfand?*" she asks increduously, and then describes at some length how she holds Siegfried's love higher than anything else, including the immortal gods by whom she herself was sired. For Brünnhilde considers Siegfried and herself in a real sense one, a unity so complete that Siegfried can say, in the Prologue to *Götterdämmerung,* that he is "but Brünnhilde's arm" (*ich bin nur Brünnhildes Arm!*). In turn, during the overwhelming conclusion of *Siegfried,* Brünnhilde had affirmed to Siegfried that "I am you yourself" (*Du selbst bin ich*). But in addition to the sheer power of love, Brünnhilde has explicitly mentioned the contractual aspect of their relationship, the ring as "love's pledge." It is as much Siegfried's pledge of love as that love itself which determines Brünnhilde's decison to value her relation to Siegfried higher than the world and the continued existence of the gods. For Brünnhilde, love and the oath of love have become commensurate in importance.

To return to Brünnhilde's monologue preceding her self-immolation, in order to review her account and understanding of Siegfried's subsequent actions: Brünnhilde has admitted that no one swore oaths (*Eide*) and made contracts (*Verträge*) more loyally than Siegfried, especially the "eternal oath" (*ewige Eide*) of fidelity he swore to her. However, Siegfried then betrayed all contracts, all oaths, and by such conduct he has betrayed true love itself (*die treueste Liebe*). It is important to note that, at this point, Brünnhilde does not distinguish between love and the institutional devices which sanctioned love—if oaths have been betrayed, then the truest love has also been betrayed. Brünnhilde's next words are therefore especially vital in expressing her final awareness of her relation to Siegfried and to Siegfried's oaths. She says that Siegfried, the "most pure," *had* to betray her in order that she might discover "wisdom" (*Mich . . . musste / der Reinste verraten, / dass wissend würde ein Weib!*).

What is this dearly won wisdom that now possesses Brünnhilde, and how did she discover it? After the intensely bitter episode with the devious Hagen, the acquisitive Gunther, and the drugged Siegfried, Brünnhilde was understandably distraught, and during the night she left her bridal chamber and wandered down to the Rhine. There she learned from the Rhinemaidens that the ring must be returned to its proper resting place. The Rhinemaidens had previously informed Siegfried of the same wisdom. They had attempted to convince him of the potential dangers of the ring by describing the harm that would come to him if he did not return it to the Rhine. But this veiled threat to his heroic character only excited Siegfried to reject their plea, after a pointless display of bravado. However, their advice, the same advice which Brünnhilde had previously rejected when conveyed to her by Waltraute, she now accepts because the coordination of values in her world has been completely shaken by recent events. Brünnhilde has become aware that the intensity of her love and the sincerity of the oaths that gave legitimacy to the expression of that love have somehow become spoiled. And "wisdom" now dictates that both the mortal lovers and the divine guardian of oaths must be expurgated by the cleansing destruction of fire.

This wisdom becomes apparent to Brünnhilde only *after* she professes the authenticity of contracts and, in particular, Siegfried's oath of love. Thus, Brünnhilde would never have been led to the fateful conclusion that Siegfried's "true" love was anything other than true unless the oaths Siegfried swore were in some crucial sense intrinsically corrupt. The presence of such corruption compels Brünnhilde to emphasize these oaths and to assert that Siegfried swore similar types of contracts. It has already been noted that Siegfried never entered a contract with anyone the way Wotan entered into a contract with the giants. But Brünnhilde here calls to mind the fact that an oath is a species of contract, and her passionate wisdom empowers her to conclude that if oaths are inauthentic and corrupt then *all* forms of contractual relation must be corrupt. Nevertheless, Brünnhilde's very last word before plunging into the fire—*Weib*—testifies how strongly the oath between the two lovers had impregnated her experience of that love. Brünnhilde is still very much a product of the epoch in which she lived as a warrior goddess and as mortal lover of Siegfried. At the moment when the epochal regime built upon contracts and oaths is on the verge of extinction, Brünnhilde still sees herself both as wife to a husband and as woman in love with a man.

Brünnhilde's lingering divinity, that divinity which had granted her prescience and the memory of her prior love for an unborn Siegfried, has now disclosed the full extent of the harm caused by the institution of contracts. Only the most drastic measures can heal the universal corruption instigated by Wotan's almost studied mismanagement of contracts, mirrored in the misadventures of mortals when they also used oaths and contracts for their own ends. Brünnhilde must therefore throw the firebrand, ignite the dessicated timbers of the ash tree surrounding Valhalla, and thereby destroy the gods by fire. This fire, and the subsequent flooding of the Rhine, will allow the regeneration of values and the establishment of new principles of order for a world that has grown too old. Eternity has now come to an end, at least the eternity that Brünnhilde felt pertained to both her love for Siegfried and the oaths sworn in defense of that love. Even Brünnhilde's truly heroic character has become too embroiled in the welter of emotional and contractual experiences that defined the complex pattern of her life as warrior and lover. She, too, must die in order that time and the world can be born again.

3

Retrospect

As the final curtain falls on *Götterdämmerung*, Wagner's stage directions indicate that "men and women" (*Männer und Frauen*) stand in spellbound horror watching the holocaust of Valhalla. Life will go on for these individuals, even though their gods and their most important institutions have now been destroyed. But what sort of post-Götterdämmerung world is suggested by the *Ring?*

In chapter 1, I maintained that one should approach the *Ring* after having introduced a fairly sharp distinction between the boundaries of art and the boundaries of life. By so doing, a serious student of the *Ring* will be compelled to discern its structure as clearly and as comprehensively as possible in terms defined solely by the symbolic world of the *Ring*. However, here in chapter 3, I wish to relax that distinction, at least to the extent of construing the *Ring* as a document that expresses a message about the world viewed independently of art. The original distinction between art and life thus becomes less sharp, but the dividend for sacrificing this sharpness is a more concrete appreciation for situating a grand but in some ways disturbing work of art within the flux of life as lived.

Even from this modified perspective, however, it should go without saying that the *Ring* is not and cannot be interpreted as a treatise in political philosophy. Such treatises are conceptually rigorous, at least in intent, and the *Ring* cannot be rigorous in this way because it is art and not philosophy. One could perhaps contend that if the interpretation takes the "realistic" direction just indicated, the interpreter's arguments should be rigorous precisely where the work of art under scrutiny is not. But I do not believe that such interpretive rigor is possible, given the vast complexity of the *Ring* as a whole and the many critical avenues that lead into and through that complexity. Accordingly, the commentary of chapter 3 is suggestive rather than definitive, both with respect to the artistic structure of the *Ring* and with respect to the concepts of political philosophy. The notions and distinctions to be developed in chapter 3 are not intended to stand by themselves as "the truth," but rather may serve collectively as a mirror in which one can see the world of the *Ring* in relation to that much more complex world which is reality.

It bears repeating that the inferences drawn below are based solely on Wagner's poem for the *Ring* and not on any of his other writings (an interpretive principle defended in chapter 1). Also, new texts from the *Ring* will be cited and texts already introduced will be cited again, a procedure required by the comprehensive scope of this retrospective view.

The Status of Contracts in the Redeemed World

The first phase of this speculative cosmological reconstruction concerns the relative importance of the divine and natural orders. It is known for certain that nature in various forms (fire, water, human beings) survives the destruction of Valhalla. But if the gods themselves are also destroyed at the conclusion of the *Ring*, does this mean that in the redeemed world there will be no gods? The theology of the *Ring* is such that the gods represent either natural forces (for instance, Froh, Freia, Loge) or institutions that became conventional after having natural origins (Fricka and Wotan). The young Wotan may have been no less divine than the mature Wotan, but had young Wotan not drunk from nature's spring and broken off the branch from nature's ash tree, young Wotan would never have become that god who was also the wise and powerful guardian of the world. Therefore, I suggest that, in general, the race of gods is divine because it is a race derived from and sustained by nature. And this derivation in turn elevates nature as such above the gods, since it is known that at least the natural elements of water and fire will continue to exist in the redeemed world after the gods who represent these elements have been destroyed. Thus, nature generates all forms of divinity—the theology of the *Ring* is more monotheistic than polytheistic, more pantheistic than anthropomorphic.

This conclusion is important. Nature will continue to exist in the redeemed world even if the gods do not. However, even if the gods do exist in this world, their existence depends on the fact that what each god represents is necessary to the natural order. If, for example, a god of fire will continue to exist in the redeemed world, one now knows that the divinity of this god depends on the fact that fire is fundamental to nature. Whether or not the fire god will resemble the anthropomorphic character of Loge becomes largely irrelevant. In fact, the question concerning the existence or nonexistence of the gods in the redeemed world is itself of secondary importance. The crucial question must be directed at nature itself, not at one of nature's forms of expression. One must inquire whether those aspects or institutions of civilized life which were natural to the corrupt world will retain that status in the redeemed world.[1]

My special interest in the context of this study concerns the institution of contracts. This institution had a natural origin and was a vital feature of the world, at least until the time when the world became corrupt after contracts and oaths had been almost systematically abused and violated. But will the institution of contracts itself survive the destruction of Valhalla? If contracts are as natural to civilized life as fire and water, then the answer is yes, contracts will in fact remain part of the redeemed world. The problem concerns whether or not the *Ring* suggests that contracts are natural to the affairs of civilized life.

At this point, my commentary strikes a bold course, but one that I believe both the letter and the spirit of the *Ring* fully warrant. I shall attempt to demonstrate that the institution of contracts will not be part of the redeemed world because that institution does, in fact, run contrary to nature despite the natural origin of that institution and its epochal duration. I shall inaugurate this particular phase of the retrospect in an indirect way by first offering an answer to one of the most vexing interpretive problems posed by the narrative of the *Ring*. The problem was noted by Wagner's contemporaries and it remains perplexing even to some recent commentators.[2] I have included the matter here because my discussion of the problem presents an answer that will also establish a framework for resolving the question concerning the status of contracts I have just raised.

The classical interpretive problem is this: Why must the gods and Valhalla be destroyed *after* the ring has been returned to the Rhinemaidens? Wagner's final and lengthy stage directions show quite clearly that the fire ignited by Brünnhilde reaches the timbers surrounding Valhalla only after the ring has found its proper resting place. But if the salvation of Wotan's divine regime depends exclusively on the return of the ring to the Rhine, then it certainly appears as though the race of gods has been destroyed without due cause.

My contention is that Wotan's pursuit of the ring as an instrument for personal aggrandizement is not as crucial as what Wotan did in the process of that pursuit. In more general terms, the downfall of the gods was necessitated not by the nature of the end that they sought, but rather by the means taken to achieve that end. Viewed in this light, the pursuit of the ring should be seen as an effect and not a cause, since the gods, acting as they did, would have been doomed regardless of the nature of that which they pursued. Therefore, the fact that the ring has been returned to the Rhine in no way mitigates the seriousness of the gods' actions in the course of seeking to control the power of the ring. Stated simply, the end does not justify the means—even when the end is the exercise of power on a cosmic scale, and the means are readily available to divinities who desire that end.

What then did the gods, especially Wotan, do to deserve their destruction? In chapter 2, I argued that Wotan became ruler of the gods and guardian of the world because of certain fundamental contractual commitments he made with sources of wisdom and power rooted in nature. Furthermore, Wotan maintained this position both by respecting these commitments and whatever other contracts he himself would subsequently enter and by overseeing the just fulfillment of all other legitimate contracts and oaths. But, as has been shown in some detail, Wotan violated his own contracts and oaths and did not punish other individuals who also violated their own contracts and oaths. One may assume that in the natural order, that which lives and thrives by contracts fulfilled decays and dies by contracts violated. Therefore, there is sufficient reason for the destruction of Valhalla and all that Valhalla represents simply by virtue of Wotan's premeditated sins against the very institution that established the basis for his position of authority. And given the divine kinship that binds the gods to one another, the just fate of one god—especially if that god is the architect and guardian of that kinship—must be shared by all other gods. All the gods must perish once it becomes necessary for one god to perish.

The golden ring fashioned by Alberich from the Rhinegold is a tangible reminder of the quest for power on the grandest scale. The pursuit of the ring by the gods, and their retreat from the ring after it has become a potential menace, should serve to focus our attention on the contractual abuses which permeated Wotan's regime during the attempt to secure the ring, as well as on other abuses of a similar sort which occurred both before and after the generation of the ring. Thus, my suggestion is that the significance of the ring as such should be determined by connecting the ring to the institution of contracts. In support of this interpretation, consider the fact that the ring *was* shunned by the gods when, in *Das Rheingold*, Wotan yielded the ring to the giants. Yet despite this literal compliance with Erda's injunction to Wotan, *Das Rheingold* concludes with the Rhinemaidens describing the race of gods as "false and fainthearted" (*falsch und feig*). Now if it is true that the gods are false *after* they have given up the ring in *Das Rheingold*, how can they be anything but false throughout the remainder of the *Ring?* My contention is that the Rhinemaidens' accusation does not concern the external manner in which the gods have conducted themselves toward the ring, but rather points to their low motivations and their base violation of contractual rights and obligations fundamental to the world order that they oversee. Wotan's behavior toward the giants and toward Alberich provides the principal source for the Rhinemaidens' recriminations. Therefore, although the ring is returned to the Rhine at the conclusion of *Götterdämmerung*, my own conclusion is that the damage to the race of gods had been wrought long before. In fact, the doom of the gods is justifiably hinted at while they mount the rainbow bridge to Valhalla at the close of *Das Rheingold*.

My answer to this problem in Wagnerian scholarship receives its impetus from the paramount importance of contracts in the *Ring*, regardless of whether the contracts concern gods or mortals. If, as I have argued, the destruction of the gods was caused by their concerted abuse of contracts, then the contractual dimension of the world prior to the Valhalla holocaust supersedes in importance even the dimension of divinity. One aspect of this superior importance comes to light when one considers the most fundamental reason why the gods were doomed. But did the destruction of the gods also include the destruction of that which the gods represented, in particular, the institution of contracts? The fact that this institution served as the ground for world order during that epoch of history under Wotan's rule is not sufficient by itself to justify the belief that contracts will automatically function in the same or even a similar way for the redeemed world. What then is the status of contracts in that world?

The matter is complex, and one can begin to answer this question only after drawing some distinctions. The first distinction concerns the significance of the destruction of Wotan's spear, on which had been carved records of contracts. Does the destruction of the spear mean (*a*) that some or perhaps all *individual* contracts were effectively corrupt, or (*b*), that the very *institution* of contracts itself was corrupt? To illustrate the force of this distinction, I may note that if (*a*) is the case, then contracts have become corrupt because of some flaw in the character of the individual or individuals who made these contracts, not because of the nature of the contractual exchange itself. If, however, (*b*) is the case, then regardless of how exemplary the character of the contractor may be, the corruption of any and every individual contract becomes inevitable by the very nature of the exchange, since it is itself corrupt. One should also note the relation between (*a*) and (*b*). The presence of an individually corrupt contract does not mean that the institution of contracts is corrupt, since, of course, contracts other than the corrupt contract may be perfectly legitimate; however, should it happen that the very institution of contracts is corrupt, then each and every individual contract will necessarily be corrupt.

In order to determine the status of contracts in the redeemed world, one must consider alternative (*b*) rather than alternative (*a*), since (*b*) is more inclusive than (*a*). Thus, if we cannot get beyond the fact that some of Wotan's individual contracts became corrupt simply because Wotan himself was corrupt, then nothing has been gained as far as the possible retention of contracts in the redeemed world is concerned. (After all, a ruler who is *not* corrupt would be perfectly capable of administering contracts justly in all cases.) However, alternative (*b*) is such that the status of contracts can be resolved with at least a measure of finality. For if the very institution of contracts is itself corrupt, that institution could hardly ground the social structure of the redeemed world, since the redeemed world would then merely duplicate precisely the same world order that eventually required the drastic purgation already detailed in the *Ring*. Therefore, my interpretation of the status of contracts in the redeemed world requires that I address alternative *(b)*—I must show that the institution of contracts is corrupt, not simply that corruption has affected individual contracts.

So much for the first distinction. The second distinction is equally important. It is now known that the point at issue concerns the corruption of the institution of contracts. But such corruption could result either because *(c)* the institution of contracts contained something that *intrinsically* corrupted that institution, or because *(d)* something *external* to the institution in its original form gradually but completely eroded that institution. Once again, one alternative outweighs the other as far as the intended goal of my interpretation is concerned. In this case, alternative *(c)* must be addressed rather than alternative *(d)*. For if the corrupt condition of the institution of contracts depends on a cause external to that institution in its original pristine form, the institution could be retained in the redeemed world on condition that the cause of erosion be eliminated. Under these circumstances, the institution of contracts would always function as it originally functioned. However, what must be shown is that the institution of contracts is, at least in part, intrinsically corrupt. Something unnatural and self-destructive permeates this institution from its very origin. All the suffering in the world of the *Ring* resulted from an essentially artificial device, its genesis shrouded in the origin of Wotan's regime and its status ultimately legitimatized only by the cumulative weight of convention and tradition.[3]

The institution of contracts is, I contend, intrinsically corrupt. The *Ring* establishes this position primarily in two places. The first passage occurs in the prologue to *Götterdämmerung*. A Norn ties the golden rope of fate to a "pine tree" *(Tanne)*. She is the first and oldest of the three Norns[4] and thus the closest, at least temporally, to the origin of that fate which the Norns collectively embody. She then explains why the weaker pine has replaced the stronger ash as the natural pole of stability for the threads of fate. The reason is straightforward: the ash tree has been sapped of its primeval strength, a condition initiated when Wotan broke off a branch of the world ash for his spear. Then, "in the course of long eons *(langer Zeiten)*, the wound consumed the wood" until finally

dürr darbte der Baum

(the withered tree died).

In addition, the spring of wisdom at which Wotan drank, a libation for which he had contractually exchanged one of his eyes, has become arid, as dry of water as the world ash is dry of sap.

Clearly the Norn speaks both literally and metaphorically, and I suggest that the appropriate translation of the allegory lies primarily in one direction. Consider the connection between the broken branch and world ash tree as a part-whole relation. One would naturally expect that a branch would die once broken off from the body of its parent tree. Such is the order of nature. But the first Norn reveals that the *whole tree* died as a result of the loss of that single branch. This eventuality would not be surprising if the world ash was, at the time, a small young tree. But if it was young at the moment when Wotan broke off a branch, how could it have survived for "long eons"? And if it was small, yet wounded mortally by the loss of the branch, how would it have grown to such an extent that (*a*) it required numerous heroes to fell its trunk, and (*b*) the trunk had sufficient girth to provide timber adequate to surround the castle of Valhalla (both these details recorded by Waltraute in act 3 of *Götterdämmerung*)? Given these conditions, the world ash must have been a large and vigorous tree when Wotan broke off a branch to serve as his spear of authority and power. Therefore, since the separation of part from whole *caused the death of the whole*, this unnatural sequence of events could have resulted only if the original separation of branch from tree was itself an unnatural rape of the normal process of nature. Although, from the standpoint of divinity, nature beneficiently bestowed both the authority and the power of Wotan's regime, nature itself was damaged by the very act through which this bestowal was conferred. And whatever emanated from this violated part of nature was necessarily doomed. Since the bestowal of natural power was achieved only by virtue of instituting contractual exchanges for orderly exercise of that power, the irreversible decay and death of nature in the form of the world ash symbolizes the corrupt and ultimately self-destructive character of the institution of contracts itself, regardless of who established individual contracts and for what purposes.

The fact that the world order dictated by Wotan's regime and the world ash itself endure for a considerable period of time and with some degree of success does not mitigate the intrinsic corruption that resulted from the unnatural damage done to the tree and to nature itself. A false step was taken when nature engendered the institution of contracts as the basis of world order. And, in retrospect, traces of this falseness appear in the very first scene of *Das Rheingold*. If the Rhinemaidens may be taken as a vocal emblem of nature, then perhaps their slipshod guardianship of nature's primeval power is symptomatic of certain weaknesses in nature, for instance, allowing part of itself (the Rhinegold) to be treated in such a way that the fundamental priority of love over power can be reversed. The fact that nature allowed the institution of contracts to order the world in a corrupt manner provides an analogous example of a natural growth that is intrinsically cancerous. Once nature has corrected this false growth through the cataclysmic purgative forces of fire and water, then the ground has been cleared for a fresh start at producing less restrictive principles of order and more expansive and diversified forms of life.

As noted, this interpretation depends on certain aspects of the first Norn's description of the genesis of the world. However, the context of this episode becomes an additional factor in establishing the persuasiveness of the interpretation. Like Erda, whose wisdom has spent itself and who has retired all but exhausted into her earthly residence, the Norns at this point in *Götterdämmerung* are recounting the past while on the very brink of their own extermination. Their fateful finitude quickly becomes apparent to them, the purveyors of fate itself. At this climactic moment in their history, surely they shall speak the truth. Thus, if the three living evocations of the administration of fate are as moribund as Erda, the mouthpiece of natural wisdom, then we may conclude that all definitive factors of this epoch have been effectively eliminated, including that one institution which established and regulated the social and legal commerce of that epoch.

The pivotal point of this interpretation turns on the eventually self-destructive relation between nature and something unnaturally formed from nature, i.e., between the ash tree and the spear. And a second example of this relation occurs in the *Ring*, one which illustrates its inherent tension perhaps even more graphically. The last words in the *Ring*, "*Zurück vom Ring!*," are uttered by the frantic Hagen as the Rhinemaidens drag him— and the ring he so passionately desires—into the depths of the raging Rhine. Hagen perishes. However, the ring remains and is returned by the Rhinemaidens to its proper resting place. Presumably the Rhinemaidens want the object of Hagen's passion not because that object is a ring, but because it is a *golden* ring. The ring is natural insofar as it is golden, just as the spear was natural insofar as it was part of an ash tree; but the gold is artificial insofar as it is a ring, just as the ash tree was artificial once part of it became fashioned into a spear. I have argued that nature (the gold) was transformed into an artifact (the golden ring) by means of a contractual agreement effected by Alberich. Only when Alberich freely exchanged the capacity to love for the capacity to dominate the world was he able to alter the natural state of the gold into the artificial state of the golden ring. Thus, the powers inherent to the ring are dependent upon the institutional device by which the gold as natural was transmuted into the ring.

To review the various powers of the gold that were unleashed after Alberich's fateful decision: The transformed gold permits the forging of the Tarnhelm, from which occur qualitative changes in visual appearance and in physical nature; Alberich becomes invisible, turns himself into a dragon, toad, etc; Fafner becomes a dragon who retains the capacity to speak; Siegfried resembles Gunther in appearance and in tone of voice. Furthermore, the Rhinemaidens (and subsequently by other characters as well) make it known that due deployment of the golden ring will place its possessor in a position to rule the world. But given the actual course of events in the *Ring*, one can never really be certain whether the ring's supposed capacity in this regard is fact or myth, since for one reason or another none of those individuals who control the ring ever come near to realizing its putative power. Presumably the ring does possess the power everyone in the drama believes it to possess. Nevertheless, the absence of reliable evidence in this regard compels one to assess the impact of the transformed gold, not in light of what it could have done but rather in terms of its actual effects. And one then notices that whatever the gold accomplished in the *Ring* was *in direct conflict with the natural order*. For, in the natural order, nothing can willfully become invisible, nothing can willfully change its physical nature, etc. And such changes represent the sum total of the gold's accomplishments.

My contention is that if the actual effects of the transformed gold are ultimately unnatural, there is good reason to believe that the potential effects of the transformed gold would be equally unnatural. The transformed gold is ultimately self-destructive for all who actually avail themselves of its powers. Therefore, if someone did attain world domination by means of the golden ring, one would be wise to expect that this individual's reign would be brief and disastrous, both to self and to the world at large. There is, of course, an important difference between the ash tree as source of the spear and the Rhinegold as source of the ring. Both the spear and the ash tree are destroyed, whereas the gold continues to exist. But this difference merely reflects the generic distinction between something living and something non-living. The gold cannot suffer the same end as the ash tree because the gold is incapable of dying. But where is the gold located at the end of the *Ring?* It is at the bottom of the Rhine, a location that is tantamount to lifelessness in that the gold will be removed from the fingers of ambitious mortals grasping for a type of control that, one may presume, is unnatural to them.

The capacity of the transformed gold to initiate and complete the quest for world domination enters into the realm of possibility solely by means of a certain contractual exchange. And this exchange results in self-destruction both for those who embrace that exchange and also for those who are involved in it only indirectly. But, aside from this dire consequence, there is another that is still more telling. For even those results of this exchange which are positive are, as has been observed, contrary to the natural order. Therefore, on the principle that the character of the product reflects the character of the process, there is good reason to believe that the contractual exchange of love for power is intrinsically unnatural. The ash tree episode concerned the institution of contracts as such whereas the Rhinegold episode concerned just an individual contract, although one of fundamental and epochal scope. But since in both cases—one universal, the other particular—

the contractual aspects result in unnatural consequences, this difference only strengthens the inclusiveness and thus the persuasiveness of the interpretation that I have put forth. Both the institution of contracts as such and one particularly crucial individual contract are, in fact, intrinsically unnatural, as shown through subtly intertwining threads of symbolism gathered from throughout the *Ring*.

The Transvaluation of Values in the Redeemed World

A civilized world is a world guided by rules. The precise nature of these rules has been and doubtless will continue to be a source of considerable disagreement, but hardly anyone would deny the need for some ruling principle of order. I have argued that the world depicted in the *Ring* has been corrupted, and unavoidably so, by the presence of the intrinsically corrupt institution of contracts. But if the *Ring* is something more than merely a picture of a doomed world, it should be possible to elicit at least an indication of how the redeemed world will be ordered. No longer will the institution of contracts ground the activity of mortals. What then will take its place?

The *Ring* suggests four possible candidates to serve as the source of order. Each of the four—power, wisdom, freedom, and love—possesses a certain philosophical respectability. Although all four have been closely connected to the institution of contracts, they have been developed in the *Ring* in such a way that each candidate may be detached and examined from the viewpoint of becoming a principle of universal order. My discussion of the four candidates has been arranged hierarchically, although the precise order of this hierarchy and the content of each step in that order must remain more or less speculative. The hierarchy I have adopted orders the four possibilities successively, according to their relative likelihood of assuming a position of preeminence in the redeemed world. As we shall see, the discussion of each candidate is such that it naturally gives rise to the discussion of its successor.

Power

By virtue of his contractual exchange with nature, Wotan possessed the greatest visible power evident in the *Ring*. Nonetheless, he craved still more power. In his own words, he wanted to become the "mightiest of mighty lords." Wotan was corrupted by sacrificing the sacred character of contracts for the sake of acquiring power, an end that he considered more important than anything else at this moment in his career. If pursuit and exercise of power were of sufficient intrinsic value, the violation of a corrupt institution to achieve that end might appear justified. However, since events have indicated that Wotan's actions with respect to that institution were not justified, regardless of its intrinsic status, there is good reason to think that power as such is not higher in value than even the dessicated institution of contracts. As a result, power will assume a position of priority in the redeemed world only if no other principle of order can take its place.

Wagner carefully and consistently presents naked power as, at best, a dubious good. The poem indicates more than once that power exercised without the guidance of wisdom results either directly or indirectly in tragedy and destruction. When, in scene 2 of *Das Rheingold*, Loge reveals the circumstances surrounding the Rhinegold's potential, he remarks that if the gold is forged into a ring, "it will help" *(hilft es)* one to attain the highest power. Although expressed subtly, the implication is surely that mere possession of the ring only partially fulfills the conditions required for achieving that power. Wotan's response to these revelations indirectly points to the implicit distinction between power as such and the wise exercise of power. His initial response is to muse that such a ring "would provide" *(schüf)* power and riches beyond measure. Wotan has heard from Loge and perhaps elsewhere as well of the power attainable from possession of the ring; he has not heard, or (since Loge has just informed him) chooses to ignore, its prerequisite—the pursuit and attainment of such power must be mediated through the guidance of wisdom.

The brief history of Alberich's ownership of the ring graphically illustrates Loge's point. Alberich exercises the power of the ring first by coercing Mime to make the Tarnhelm and then by showing off its distinctive properties to his divine visitors, Loge and Wotan. But Alberich lacks discretion and foresight; as a result, his reign with the ring, hardly reaching the pinnacle that he had sought, is almost comically brief. Had his wisdom been as extensive as his power, he would never have placed himself in a position where the theft of the ring could have been accomplished with such ease.

The subordination of power to wisdom reoccurs later when the *Ring* approaches its climax. In act 1 of *Götterdämmerung*, Hagen tells Gunther that "in truth, the world would bow to whoever knew how to use" the ring well *(Wer wohl ihn zu nützen wüsst; / dem neigte sich wahrlich die Welt)*. Hagen repeats the point that mere possession of the ring does not guarantee the successful attainment of the end for which the ring was first fashioned. One must know how to use the ring wisely before it can become truly effective rather than, as it was for Alberich, merely a display piece permitting its owner a certain degree of superficial and temporary control. Although power without wisdom is certainly attainable in a corrupt world, the exercise of such power works only to the disadvantage of its possessor.

In fact, the tragic repercussions of power without wisdom extend not only to those who actually possess the ring, but also to those who merely crave it and even to those who neither possess nor crave, but who are in the presence of those who do. And, of course, this presence includes everyone in the world. Waltraute has affirmed that the dire effects of the ring are world-wide—"the world's ills spring from it." The various problems that beset Alberich, Wotan, Fafner, Mime, and Hagen in their respective quests for the ring and the resultant varieties of evil they engender burgeon into a cancerous malignancy. As a result, the pursuit of power simply for power's sake must be considered as an infection serious enough to destroy a world.

Wisdom

If power must be guided by wisdom even in a corrupt and ultimately doomed world order, wisdom is at least equivalent to and probably greater than power as far as intrinsic value is concerned. But wisdom in the unredeemed world was, in its own way, no less riddled with imperfection than the power that should have been under its aegis. Wisdom is represented anthropomorphically by Erda and her three daughters, the Norns. Erda is "primevally wise"; she knows the past, present, and future, and with the Norns weaves this wisdom into the golden rope of fate. But during Erda's first appearance in the *Ring*, the information she conveys to Wotan in *Das Rheingold* is curiously ambivalent, in a sense even unwise. Thus, in retrospect, the finitude of her wisdom is manifest in her very first pronouncements. She warns of the danger to the gods' existence and suggests by the tone of the warning, if not by its literal content, that perhaps the danger can be averted if the proper steps are taken. She then advises Wotan to "shun the ring," presumably a necessary condition for the gods' preservation.

As already noted, Wotan does heed this warning; he shuns the ring in the sense that he yields possession of it to the giants, once he has been pressured into fulfilling his contract with them. But it should be made clear that Erda, the voice of wisdom, does not tell Wotan to return the ring to the Rhine, the only "natural" remedy for the ring's accursed condition. Wotan is aware from Loge's frequent exhortations that the Rhinemaidens have been pleading for the ring to be returned to them. But the point is that Erda's wisdom was either intrinsically deficient or etched with deviousness. And since Wotan has more reason to listen to Erda than to secondhand reports concerning the wishes of the Rhinemaidens, the wisdom made available to him at this particularly crucial juncture, and by the official spokesman for that wisdom, was hardly as percipient as one would have expected.

Erda's cryptic warning coupled with the loss of the much-desired ring only fires Wotan's ambition and his curiosity. During the interval between the end of the dramatic action of *Das Rheingold* and the beginning of the dramatic action of *Die Walküre*, Wotan descended into the depths of the earth and then, by the magic of love, enticed Erda to reveal what she knew. Presumably Wotan now knows all that Erda knows. Thus, if Erda knows the past and the future, Wotan also knows the past and the future. In his guise as the Wanderer, Wotan testifies to his knowledge of the inexorability of events in the frequently cited remark in act 2 of *Siegfried: "Alles ist nach seiner Art."* The "way" in which "all things are" includes both past and future events. Therefore, this necessity also includes the curse on the ring, which, although activated by Alberich at a definite point in time, was actually coincident with the creation of the present world order. During the Rhinemaidens' playful inquisition of Siegfried in *Götterdämmerung*, they describe how the curse was woven into the "rope of primeval and eternal law" *(in des Urgesetzes ewiges Seil)*, then remained quiescent until someone contractually exchanged love for the capacity to acquire and exercise power. But if Wotan knows the past and the future to the extent that Erda knows the past and future, he also knows of his own eventual demise and of the necessary destruction of Valhalla. Why then did he attempt to save himself and his regime? In addition to the reasons already proposed in chapter 2, it may have been simply because Erda's wisdom appeared to him shallow, perhaps even capable of circumvention. But regardless of the reason for Wotan's subjective reaction, true wisdom should instill in its recipient a desire to act on the basis of that wisdom. Since Wotan did not act on the basis of what he had learned from Erda's wisdom, such wisdom was deficient as far as projecting its character as truth into the stimulus for right conduct. And if wisdom is deficient at its source, then it will become all the more attenuated when it becomes incorporated into the individual deeds of those mortals and gods who have acted according to its lights.

The deterministic principle that all things are according to their own way extends to the origin and voice of wisdom itself. In the first scene of act 3 of *Siegfried*, the Wanderer proclaims to a sleepy Erda that her wisdom is "coming to an end" *(geht zu Ende)*. Erda shrugs off her own impending fate, an appropriate reaction for a wise being who senses that her term of existence has run its allotted course. Nevertheless, her period of dominance, emblematic of epochal wisdom, is about to end. Thus, in the prologue to *Götterdämmerung*, the Norns chorus in unison *"Zu End' ewiges Wissen!"* The Norns are Erda's progeny, and they derive their respective functions as the instruments of fate from the direction of Erda's wisdom. But if the representative of natural wisdom is no longer eternal, then the Norns' determination of future events will be marked by the finitude of their maternal origin. The accuracy of fate depends on the reliability of the wisdom that underlies fate.

Erda manifests her moribund condition by her comatose appearance, but the Norns reveal their commensurate state of decay in a more subtle way. The Norns' principal role is to state and fulfill prophecy, and Wagner skillfully delineates their prophetic deficiencies through details of speech and staging. Thus, the world ash tree from which Wotan had broken the branch of contractual power has been hewn to pieces—now a pine tree has replaced the ash as the central point of focus for the Norns' rope of fate. But the pine is no match for the ash as far as strength and resiliency are concerned, and this natural difference symbolizes the difference between the strength of wisdom past and the pliancy of wisdom present. Also, the first Norn admits that she can no longer "see plainly" *(nicht hell)*, and the third Norn foresees *Wotan* throwing the firebrand onto the timber surrounding Valhalla. The first Norn's admission of growing prophetic blindness culminates in the third Norn's serious misreading of future events. For it is Brünnhilde, not Wotan, who will ignite the logs, thereby initiating the destruction of Valhalla and the "eternal" gods. Had Wotan acted as prophesized by the third Norn, he would have fulfilled at least part of his original wish to be the active force willing the gods' destruction. But Brünnhilde, Erda's "child of wisdom" *(wissendes Kind)*, will perform this world-redeeming act—not Wotan. The fact that the third Norn foresees what Wotan had intended to do, as opposed to what in fact will occur, suggests the intimacy between natural wisdom and divine interests. But the main point here is that the Norns have lost the power of accurate prophecy, just as Erda has lost the wisdom to substantiate the rightness of conduct, both mortal and divine, and just as Wotan has lost both the reality and the appearance of authority and power.

In general, power and wisdom may serve either as ends in themselves or as means to achieve other ends. But regardless of how power and wisdom are intrinsically and instrumentally related to each other and to other ultimate values, their nature in the corrupt world is described in such a way that both must be placed in a state of suspension as far as their potential role in the redeemed world is concerned. In the *Ring*, all those who pursue power for power's sake are destroyed by that pursuit. Therefore, power without wisdom is self-destructive, a state that probably applies just as much to the redeemed world as to the corrupt world. But wisdom, whether invoked during the quest for power or for any other end, is, if not self-destructive, at least of finite duration. In fact, in this particular epoch, wisdom as embodied by Erda and the Norns becomes completely hollow and eventually dies away altogether. One must assume that power and wisdom will reappear in the redeemed world, but their status in the corrupt world is such that individual actions in the redeemed world based on these values will originate from different motivations and therefore bear a more elevated moral quality. Thus, power will be pursued—if at all—for reasons other than self-aggrandizement (Wotan) and tyrranical control (Alberich). One may conclude that neither power nor wisdom are of sufficient stature to span the gap between the corrupt world now purged and the redeemed world at hand.

Freedom

A wise man who must act within the boundaries of a corrupt institution can hardly be expected to manifest his wisdom. For even if it should happen that he truly possessed wisdom of the highest order, his actions would be unavoidably affected by the corrupt circumstances within which he must lead his life. In general, those individuals held in bondage by some force or institution can realize what remains of their nature to the extent that they can separate themselves from these harmful restrictions. Now in the corrupt world, all principal characters in the *Ring* were restricted to some degree by their contractual agreements. The primary source of that restriction may be located at the very heart of the nature of any contractual exchange. For to enter a contract entails an obligation to fulfill that contract. And obligation of this sort becomes, in a sense, a restriction on freedom, since an individual obliged to do something is not free not to do that thing. However, perhaps this kind of restriction on freedom became essential to the world of the *Ring* only because that world was imperfect in its origin and in its development.

According to this line of thought, the very presence of contractual obligation became an unavoidable restriction on natural freedom. But since the redeemed world will no longer be controlled by the institution of contracts, the principle of obligation will no longer be present, at least in the form in which that principle animated the institution of contracts. The inhabitants of the redeemed world will neither need nor desire contracts because their interactions will be ordered by some naturally less restrictive principle than that imposed by the institution of contracts and the obligation essential to that institution. Therefore, perhaps the principle of order will be some form of that freedom now present to a human nature no longer encumbered by contractual obligations.

Freedom (*frei* and cognates) is a term which appears in a number of highly diverse and important contexts in the *Ring*. Before beginning to consider these contexts, it should be noted that as soon as the term "free" departs from loose popular or even more elevated aesthetic usage and is taken to approach some sort of rigorous meaning, it becomes extremely difficult to define. This problem will also apply to the usages of the term "free" in the *Ring*. My procedure will be to examine pertinent examples of the term in several contexts and then to attempt a general formulation of freedom in the *Ring* as a whole.

a. *Erda*. With one exception, the term freedom is ascribed to all levels of the *Ring's* cosmology. That exception is Erda. But Erda differs qualitatively from god, man, giant, dwarf, and even another nature-entity, the Rhinemaidens. Since, by her very nature, Erda must disseminate wisdom, she of course cannot be free with respect to the limits of knowledge. Erda can neither learn nor forget—she knows what she knows and in this respect is fully determinate. She may elect to appear to Wotan at a certain point in the history of his regime; in this sense she is free. But she cannot be free to alter what she knows about the history of that regime, both its past and its future. Therefore, the fact that Erda is not explicitly connected with the notion of freedom does not tell against the importance of freedom either in the world of the *Ring* or in the redeemed world.

b. *Wotan*. In *Das Rheingold*, Wotan displays the extent of his power. He swiftly and forcefully halts the impending skirmish between Donner and Fasolt over Freia, thus proving his earlier claim that he has no need to call for assistance when his own "free courage" *(freier Mut)* can prevail. But from another and more important perspective, Wotan is not at all free, and he knows that he is not free long before Valhalla and its inhabitants have been consumed in flames. Thus, after his bitter colloquy with Fricka in *Die Walküre*, he cries that he is the "most unfree of all" *(ich Unfreiester aller!)*. And later, during the lengthy peroration before he kisses away Brünnhilde's divinity, Wotan proclaims that only one who is "freer than I, the god" *(freier als ich, der Gott!)* will win Brünnhilde for his bride.

Wotan is not free because he has become slave to the very contracts that had originally made him master. As a result, an individual "free of the gods' favor" *(frei seiner Gunst)* must appear in order to counteract Alberich's threat to end shamefully the divine dynasty. Since Wotan himself is not free, he can engender only "slaves" *(Knechte)*, albeit slaves characterized by a certain nobility, for instance, Siegmund. "I cannot will a free being" *(Einen Freien kann ich nicht wollen)* he laments to Brünnhilde. Only when he has been transformed from Wotan to the Wanderer can he "now freely perform" *(führe frei ich nun aus)* what had caused him endless anguish earlier—the establishment of conditions that allow the generation of a hero who can will to do what Wotan himself cannot. But that very hero will effectively terminate the Wanderer's reign, thus eliminating even the possibility that Wotan could restore himself to that level of freedom he once so grandly displayed.

c. *Brünnhilde*. Wotan's daughter Brünnhilde appears to be free in precisely the sense in which Wotan is not. Of her own accord, she alters, although only temporarily, the pre-ordained outcome of Siegmund's combat with Hunding. Her action, in direct disobedience to Wotan's command, was instigated because she had been struck so deeply by Siegmund's "most free love" *(freiester Liebe)* for Sieglinde. But is her involvement the simple result of pure free choice? There is textual evidence to the contrary. When Wotan claims that Brünnhilde is "free" *(frei)* to choose as she wishes, Fricka quickly responds that this claim is not true and that Brünnhilde merely "fulfills your will" *(deinen Willen / vollbringt)*. And just prior to Wotan's monologue, Brünnhilde herself says, "Who am I if I am not your will?" *(wer bin ich, / wär ich dein Wille nicht?)*. When she initially refuses to obey his command that Siegmund be slain, Wotan himself describes her in this way, using even more

forceful language: "Who are you other than the blind instrument of my will?"
And again, later, before he strips her godhead for disobeying that command:
"You live through my will alone." This testimony, from both Brünnhilde and
Wotan, makes it doubtful whether Brünnhilde is acting freely and of her own
accord when she attempts to intervene on Siegmund's behalf. Rather, she is
carrying out, as an extension of Wotan's hidden will, a wish that he would
execute himself but cannot because he has sworn an oath to Fricka to avenge
the marriage contract broken by the two lovers.

If Brünnhilde is indeed an "eternal part" *(ewig Teil)* of Wotan, then
presumably she can become free only when she has been freed from Wotan's
own condition of bondage. Thus, when she realizes that her divinity is about
to end, she begs Wotan to protect her so that only a "fearless most free hero"
(furchtlos / freiester Held) shall discover and claim her in marriage. She
knows, at least intuitively, that her own existence will be worth preserving
only on condition that the hero who awakens her will possess a type of
freedom that she lacked and that she could not participate in as long as her
quasi-divine nature remained determined by her relation to Wotan. But
Brünnhilde must endure much more before she finally learns the true
meaning of freedom. Only when she removes the ring from the finger of the
dead Siegfried does she proclaim: "All things I know, all these things now
make me free!" *(Alles weiss ich, / Alles ward mir nun frei!)*. But the
awareness of this freedom leads directly to Brünnhilde's self-immolation and
to the act that initiates the public destruction of the regime of which she was
once an integral part. It is an evanescent freedom, at least in its initial
emergence within this erstwhile divinity now doomed to share the fate of a
world that lacked such freedom.

d. *Siegfried*. Brünnhilde's awareness of freedom results from the actions of
Siegfried, unfortunate though these actions may be for both lovers. But to
what extent is Siegfried himself free? Brünnhilde has referred to the individual who will awaken her from her divinely induced sleep as "most free." That
individual is Siegfried. When does Siegfried achieve this state of freedom?
According to his own testimony, "I became free" *(ich frei ward)* after he
decides to forge the sword Nothung from the remnants given to him by
Mime. In making this decision and in forging the sword in his artless but
effective way, Siegfried fulfills Wotan's injunction, announced to Brünnhilde
in the act 2 monologue of *Die Walküre*, that "the free man must create
himself" *(selbst muss der Freie sich schaffen)*. Once Siegfried has forged his
sword, he will freely terminate Wotan's rule by shattering the Wanderer's
spear. He will then freely learn the meaning of fear. However, Siegfried's
freedom and the deeds he performs consequent upon this freedom eventually lead to his death at the hand of Hagen. And Brünnhilde's freedom also
leads to her death, but as the result of an awareness—won at great price—

that compelled her to die of her own accord and for the sake of a greater good. Whatever its precise nature may be, such freedom is hardly mere flippancy—its effects range over the full spectrum of life and death, for hero and heroine alike.

e. *The Dwarves*. The effect of freedom is not restricted to the conduct of divinities and mortals. It applies to dwarves as well. In scene 4 of *Das Rheingold*, Loge advises Alberich that "no free man makes amends for the evil-doer" *(büsst kein Freier den Frevel)*, implying that one who acts freely will not act in a favorable manner toward one who is bound by evil. And Alberich forthrightly declares that he "freely" *(frei)* sinned against himself by foresaking love for power, in contrast to Wotan, who sinned against the very source of his own authority when he stole the ring from Alberich. In addition, Alberich's fellow dwarf Mime, his brother and rival, muses on the possibility that one day Alberich shall be in thrall to the "free one" *(Freien)*, Mime, who at that time was still subject to Alberich. Although the dwarves are uniquely different from both gods and men, they nonetheless have the capacity to be just as affected by freedom or the lack of freedom as their mortal and immortal counterparts.

f. *The Giants*. In the second scene of *Das Rheingold*, Fasolt refers to the giants as a "free" race, originally bound by Wotan to peace *(bandest uns Frei / zum Frieden du)*. However, this peace will be threatened if Wotan does not "honorably and freely" *(ehrlich und frei)* fulfill his end of the contract for the construction of Valhalla. The reason Wotan was originally able to coerce the giants by means of contracts into a state of relative submission is not given. But the giants, although they may now be "clods," are by no means insensitive to their heritage. The giants were once free, and because they retain at least a vestige of that freedom, they call on Wotan the god to act in the present as a free race of giants had once acted in the past. They insist that Wotan freely accept what in any case he is morally and legally obligated to honor, his end of the contract. For a once-free race no longer free, the principal sources of liberation or advancement are guile and force. And since the giants lack guile (although Fasolt less so than Fafner), they must force Wotan to comply with the contract by taking as hostage Freia, the source of the gods' youth. But their hopes for achieving wealth and social advancement are without substance. The giants are fated to suffer the same end as all others who sacrifice higher values for the acquisition of power and its trappings. Fasolt is killed by Fafner; Fafner is killed by Siegfried.

g. *The Rhinemaidens*. Like Erda, the Rhinemaidens embody properties of nature as well as the anthropomorphic characteristics displayed in their dealings with dwarves, heroes, and gods. Thus, the Rhinemaidens may be seen as intermediating between nature as such and human nature. Although the Rhinemaidens do not exemplify all that is fine in human nature, their position as intermediator, if conjoined with an expression of freedom, should reveal something of the extent to which nature is capable of instituting freedom within the limits of anthropomorphic conduct.

In the third act of *Götterdämmerung*, Siegfried meets the Rhinemaidens. They ask him to return the ring. At first he refuses, but the sharpness of their taunts persuades him to give up the ring. At this point, however, the Rhinemaidens are no longer playful. They grimly advise Siegfried to keep the ring, guard it, and learn for himself of the ring's unholiness. They tell Siegfried how glad he will be when they finally "free" *(befrein)* him from the curse placed on the ring. As events will show, Siegfried becomes free from the curse only after the immoral character of his sworn oaths has been duly reckoned. Since his final oath is ostensibly marked by perjury, Siegfried's liberation will require that his life be sacrificed to the point of Hagen's spear. However, if Siegfried had returned the ring at the proper moment, the Rhinemaidens would have freed him from the curse at no apparent cost to his well-being, much less at the extreme price of his life. But what Siegfried does or does not do need not concern one in this context. The point is that the Rhinemaidens represent the capacity for releasing a mortal, and a heroic mortal, from a curse that springs from the most fundamental sources of power and obligation. Although their guardianship of the Rhinegold was slack, they have not by their remiss conduct in that case lost the potential of conferring a type of freedom that can subsequently be established only by purging an entire world order. But as this episode seems to indicate, nature as represented by the Rhinemaidens will not readily yield the capacity for such freedom.

h. *Nature.* Although Siegfried's promise of freedom is announced to him by the Rhinemaidens, they are the medium rather than the source of that freedom. The Rhinemaidens have been empowered to act as freedom-bestowing mediators only because their very nature intimately connects them with the gold and its natural habitat. If only the gold were returned to its proper resting place, sing the Rhinemaidens, the gold would shine like a "free star of the deep" *(freier Stern der Tiefe).* Already at the conclusion of *Das Rheingold*, the Rhinemaidens had proclaimed to divine but deaf ears that only when the gold shines "in the deep" *(in der Tiefe)* will it be "true" *(treu).* The Rhinegold, now accursed, becomes free when its potential for aggravating a cosmic conflict between love and power has been eliminated in the cleansing waters of the Rhine. Once in its place, the gold will shine, a "free star," its literal location in the watery depths combined metaphorically with an appropriate heavenly brilliance. Opposites are united in this evocative image, with its harmony and distance an indication of the true natural relation between the primeval forces of love and power. All attempts to dislodge the gold and artfully but mistakenly to transform it into a ring will instigate a collision between these two forces, and the result will be as fundamental—and as cataclysmic—as these forces themselves.

My brief survey of "freedom" contexts is now complete. This constellation of contexts doubtless includes many different and perhaps even conflicting shades of meaning for its one constant, the term freedom. But the relevant meanings may be sorted out by first distinguishing between two broad senses of freedom: freedom *from* and freedom *to*. Freedom *from* implies that certain conditions in an individual's situation restrict the development of that individual's nature—thus, the state in which these restrictions have been eliminated is freedom, at least in some minimal sense. Freedom *to* implies that an individual is capable of performing types of action that may either realize or stultify his nature. When applied to the complex network of contexts outlined above, this distinction allows us to examine whether or not the principal characters have been restricted, how they have been restricted, and what they are free to be and to become once these restrictions have been removed.

The negative sense of freedom (freedom *from*) is readily determined. Wotan is unfree precisely because he owes his position of authority to the institution of contracts and cannot willfully break those contracts or withdraw from the aegis of the institution. Brünnhilde is bound to Siegfried by an oath, a type of contract, and she offers information leading to Siegfried's death because she feels certain Siegfried has broken that oath. Only when she knows more of the circumstances underlying Siegfried's actions does she proclaim herself free of the restrictions caused by her submission to the conventional dominance of the institution of contracts. Siegfried swears an oath of fidelity to Brünnhilde, is induced magically to forget that oath, contracts two more oaths and by the letter of these oaths perjures himself, and then is executed for his unholy lie. Siegfried, the destroyer of the spear representing Wotan's contractually based authority, becomes entangled in circumstances such that he can be freed only by death, circumstances strung together by a series of oaths. Alberich desires love, but foreswears it in exchange for power. His brief reign while in control of the ring comes about by means of that institution which could empower such a contractual exchange. The giants, once free, now accomplish their ends through contracts. But they can enforce such contracts only by a crude form of bartering. Their mutual destruction results from their overweening desires (Fasolt for love of a goddess, Fafner for power over the gods), desires that appear within their grasp because in the unredeemed world the institution of contracts universally binds all levels of consciousness. The Rhinemaidens are reduced from playful nymphs to distraught guardians because they were entrusted with an object that, in a sense, grounds two ultimate but very distinct values. In this case, however, love and power come into conflict when one is contractually exchanged for the other. The Rhinegold, after it has been transmuted into the ring, initiates this conflict. Although freedom can be ascribed to the Rhinegold itself, it becomes an instrument capable of interfering with the freedom of all who pursue its hidden power, given that the gold has been torn from its natural setting and then refashioned by a contractual exchange. The gold will shine just as brightly in the depths of the Rhine after ceasing to be an instrument that occasioned an epochal clash between love and power.

This brief review of the *Ring's* cosmological hierarchy shows how its principal components are directly or indirectly affected, and affected detrimentally, by the institution of contracts. Therefore, in brief, the unredeemed world must be free of that institution before life in the redeemed world, especially human life, can attain its full potential. The sustained and intimate connection throughout the *Ring* between freedom and the institution of contracts only intensifies our awareness of the intrinsically destructive quality of contracts and oaths. At the end of the *Ring*, however, the world has been freed of this institution by the natural cleansing forces of fire and water. Dawn has risen on a world now based on new principles of order.

It would, however, be extremely naive to believe that this negative sense of freedom will suffice to order an entire world. The fact that a world has been freed *from* one debilitating institution does not preclude the possibility that this world will still be subject to other forms of abuse. For example, what would prevent a potential thief from thinking that he is "free" *to* take something he desires, simply because he desires to possess that thing? The freedom to desire something does not imply that one has the right to take the object of that desire if that object belongs to another. In this and all other instances of injustice, the would-be perpetrator is free *to* perform such actions only in an anarchical world, a world lacking any principles of order. Therefore, if the redeemed world is not anarchical, then some positive principle or principles for directing human conduct must be determined. This source of moral direction must not only guide all the ways in which humans are free to act for their own self-realization, but it must also establish guidelines for determining when actions are detrimental to that realization, whether to the self of the person acting or to the self of the person acted upon.

Love

Our speculation culminates in a brief discussion of a principle that seems to insure the transition from negative freedom to positive freedom, from a freedom that eliminates intrinsic restrictions to a freedom that provides direction for human conduct. I suggest that the abstractness and incompleteness of negative freedom can be fulfilled by that "powerful love" (*mächtigster Minne*) which inflames Brünnhilde's spirit with an intensity surpassing the heat of the fire into which she has thrown herself. Love will become the fundamental principle of the new world order. The world has been redeemed *by* Brünnhilde's individual love and *for* the universal application of love in all worldly affairs. Under this interpretation, love and freedom become ultimate and correlative values, each in its own way necessary to direct human behavior. One cannot love unless one is free to love; thus, freedom is a necessary condition for the possibility of love. But if one is free, one must still act according to a principle that guarantees the realization of one's nature. Love fulfills that potential opened up by the presence of freedom.

A burden of considerable weight has been placed on love. For love must either replace other types of interpersonal relation or, preserving these other relations, elevate them so that they become based on motives instigated by love and not bare self-interest. Consider an obvious example, one drawn from the core of the *Ring*'s narrative. The redeemed world lacks the institution of contracts. Love must therefore generate the kind of mutual understanding and trust that guarantees that transactions traditionally requiring contractual sanctions (business matters, marriage, etc.) are no less binding by virtue of love than they were (in the unredeemed world) by virtue of contractual obligation. But is the serious Wagnerite to leave the *Ring* thinking that if only love were all, then two businessmen will naturally "love" each other to the point where a contract sealing a business transaction between them becomes completely superfluous, if not an overt limitation on their nature as human beings? Speculative redemptive vision now begins to fade into a utopian dream.

What then are the attributes that love at this especially fundamental level must exhibit? The *Ring* itself suggests only two instances of love suitable for the extrapolation of such attributes. Wotan and Fricka are married, but their lack of offspring intimates that passionate love did not dominate their relationship. Wotan engenders Brünnhilde and the other Valkyries by subduing Erda through a form of magical love, but surely love controlled by magic cannot be love in the sense required. Alberich sires Hagen by a mortal woman named Grimheld, but this union simply mixed carnal lust and envy in order to spawn a mortal agent necessary for the attainment of the object of that envy. Thus, when Hagen speaks of love between himself and his father, such love hardly swells with virtue. The only two instances of love that can serve as potential paradigms for future mortal interrelations are, first, the love between Siegmund and Sieglinde, and second, the love between Siegfried and Brünnhilde. Although, as noted, both relations embraced the contractual device of a marital oath, this need was due primarily to the fact that both relations transpired in a corrupt world. But the love manifested in these relations need not have been as corroded as the oaths that sanctioned that love.

The principal characteristics common to those two love relations were: Physical and spiritual passion, self-sacrifice to the point of accepting death for the sake of the loved one, and the realization of the pre-eminence of love in relation to other ultimate values. The question at hand then becomes whether or not these characteristics can be adapted to cover other apparently different but equally fundamental types of interpersonal relations. Consider the relation between two men who have fulfilled a business transaction. Perhaps these two individuals fulfilled this transaction simply because they felt obligated to do so. But obligation of this sort can be called "love" only if love is diluted to the point of becoming indistinguishable from the kind of bond that allows business transactions to be accomplished successfully. Surely the nature of love would be lost if extended in this way. Furthermore, obligation may well become a value distinct from love but just as essential as love for purposes of initiating order into the complex sphere of human relationships.

Earlier, the suggestion was made that obligation, at least as it emerged within the institution of contracts, was inherently restrictive. Now, however, one begins to suspect that this position on the negative effects of obligation may have been premature. For in view of the example concerning business matters just raised, the doctrine that love is *the* fundamental principle of the redeemed world becomes problematic. The problem may be stated in the form of a dilemma: If, on the one hand, love as defined according to the standards of intensity found in the *Ring* is intended to cover all types of interpersonal relationships, then love in this sense becomes diffuse to the point of losing its uniqueness, for instance, when the hypothetical successful business transaction is considered. But, on the other hand, if acting solely from a sense of obligation is a definitive aspect of human conduct, then obligation is no less fundamental than love for ordering human affairs, even in a redeemed world.

The doctrine of love has been subjected to criticism by confronting it with a pedestrian example drawn from a type of human conduct that will surely be part of the redeemed world, just as it was part of the corrupt world. The point of the criticism articulated by the dilemma posed above was to suggest that obligation should perhaps be restored, so that it assumes a place of funda-mental importance in the redeemed world. In fact, however, one need not go outside the definition of love derived from the *Ring* to detect the need for obligation of some sort. For regardless of the intensity of love, there are situations when a lover must act toward the beloved not from outwardly plain passion but rather from obligation, as in those cases when choosing the right course of action conflicts with a course of action that, in the heat of passionate love, appears to be mutually beneficial. True love generates a type of obligation that remains quiet when all else is tumultuous, reserved for those occasions when it is most needed, for example, where only a right action can preserve love against threats to its very existence. The obligation found in love is, of course, not nearly as detached as that present in a successful business deal, but the point is that it should be distinguished from those aspects of love which are circumscribed within the extremes of passion, a distinction that the doctrine of love under scrutiny appears to overlook.

This criticism is certainly not intended to demean the possibility that love in the sense defined may serve as the fundamental principle of world order. A world ruled by such love as the fulfillment of freedom may be utopian, but it is a far cry from a world afflicted by sheer anarchy. Perhaps the real problem concerns not so much inherent weaknesses in the notion of love, but rather the degrees of complexity that will pertain to human affairs in the redeemed world. For if this world approximates the Garden of Eden in simplicity, then the freedom to love and the activity of loving will be completely sufficient to cover all types of human conduct. Life would be a mirror image of paradise. But can human nature ever be redeemed to such a degree of perfection? In art, perhaps—in real life, one can only remain sceptical.

Concluding Remark

My retrospective view of the *Ring* is now complete. Let me conclude by listing five propositions that would seem to apply to the nature and organization of the redeemed world: (1) all values instrumental in the governance of human affairs, however these values may be defined, will originate entirely from nature; (2) these values will be directed toward the fulfillment of all levels of human consciousness; (3) a natural law will arrange these values according to an ordered priority, with all human institutions developed from these values similarly ordered; (4) violations of this natural law, whether by reversing any of its priorities or by uprooting the entire hierarchy at its source, will lead to drastic and perhaps calamitous consequences for both the violator and for the world at large; (5) this natural law will, however, be epochal in duration, since the finitude of all things natural applies to the ordering principle as well as to that which is ordered by that principle.

In general, only the primeval forces of nature will continue to roll on and on, since the institutional "wheels" that differentiate these forces and allow them to assume visible form and direction are necessarily of finite duration. *Der Ring des Nibelungen* represents one such wheel, with the corrupt world turning slowly but inexorably into a redeemed world, the nature of which has been briefly sketched. Could one survive in such a world? Would one be able to seek and achieve happiness if world redemption assumed the form inti- mated by the *Ring?* To answer these questions, one must extend the philo- sophical dimension of the *Ring* beyond the limits within which such speculation is worthwhile. As a result, any further inquiry concerning the organizational principles and details of the redeemed world would be little more than guesswork. It perhaps bears repeating that, from a strictly philosophical perspective, none of the notions introduced in this retrospect have been even correctly formulated, much less treated in such a way as to solve the many problems that result from their introduction. This result, in some ways unsatisfactory, should not be surprising; although these problems may originate in the process of an aesthetic analysis, they inevitably become philosophical issues of primary importance and considerable difficulty.

Nevertheless, the extent to which the *Ring* does reveal, or at least suggest, the true relation between natural institutions and nature as such measures the extent to which Wagner can be considered both artist and philosopher, and the *Ring* both a work of art and an implicit although provocative philosophical commentary on issues that concern everyone. And yet, however philosophically perceptive the *Ring* may be, it must remain in the final analysis a work of art. But if experienced from a number of perspectives— some concrete in their immediacy, others more abstract, it is a work of art that cannot help but lift its audience to a more sensitive awareness of what art can become as a fusion of emotion and thought.

Notes

Chapter 1. The Wagnerian Libretto

1. Ernest Newman, *Wagner as Man and Artist* (New York: Random House, 1924), p. 323.

2. Richard Wagner, *Sämmtliche Schriften und Dichtungen* (Leipzig: Breitkopf & Härtel, 1911), 4: 175–76. English translation in Richard Wagner, *Collected Prose Works*, trans. W. A. Ellis (New York: Broude Brothers, 1872–79), 2: 318–19.

3. All translations are my own. Wagner's poetic German is averse to translation because of its terseness and concerted use of alliteration and assonance. For this reason, I believe the presence of the original German is valuable, especially in an interpretation of the *Ring* based primarily on Wagner's poem, and I have included the relevant German words or phrases in the passages cited. The translations are as literal as possible.

4. The leitmotifs are named variously by different commentators. For example, this motif has also been designated as the "spear" leitmotif. But I prefer to name it by the institution the spear represents rather than by the symbol for that institution. Although the spear is tangible, whereas the institution of contracts is not, the institution supersedes the spear in ultimate importance.

5. Friedrich Nietzsche, "Richard Wagner in Bayreuth" in *Werke in Drei Bänden*, ed. Karl Schlechta (Munich: Carl Hanser Verlag, 1966), 1: 415.

6. Thomas Mann, *Essays of Three Decades*, trans. H. T. Lowe-Porter (New York: Alfred A. Knopf, 1947), p. 317.

7. Newman, *Wagner the Man*, p. 320.

8. Mann, *Essays*, p. 315.

9. Ernest Newman, *The Life of Richard Wagner* (London: Cassell, 1937), 2: 332.

10. In vol. 2 of *The Life of Richard Wagner* (p. 306), Newman points out that Mime tells Siegfried that Sieglinde "gave" (*gab*) the pieces of Siegmund's sword to him, Mime, but later Mime tells the Wanderer that he had "stolen" (*gestohlen*) the fragments of the sword. Thus, critical judgments concerning Mime's greed and ambition will depend on whether in fact he passively received or actively stole the pieces of the sword.

11. Ibid., p. 333. Wagner wrote this important and lengthy letter to his close friend August Roeckel on 25 January 1854. It is cited several times in the works on the *Ring* by George Bernard Shaw and Robert Donington. For the complete letter, see Richard Wagner, *Sein Leben in Briefen*, ed. Carl Siegmund Benedict (Leipzig: Breitkopf & Härtel, 1913), pp. 169–86.

12. Shaw makes substantially the same point when he contends that "if the *Ring* says one thing, and a letter written afterwards says that it said something else, The *Ring* must be taken to confute the letter just as conclusively as if the two had been written by different hands." George Bernard Shaw, *The Perfect Wagnerite*, 4th ed. (New York: Dover, 1967), p. 101. Robert Donington echoes the point with respect to strictly musical relations among the leitmotifs, many of which relations Wagner himself "will have not even have noticed. . . ." Robert Donington, *Wagner's "Ring" and Its Symbols*. 3d ed. (New York: St. Martin's Press, 1974), p. 275.

13. Here is a pertinent example of contradictory conclusions drawn by two different authors, each of whom spent considerable time and energy studying all of Wagner's writings. Maurice

Boucher states that although Wagner "declared himself a vanguard revolutionist," in fact "he never desired anything other than a return of a very old social state, still undifferentiated." But then compare Robert Gutman's claim, that "Wagner always remained essentially a monarchist and an authoritarian." Now if Wagner was a "monarchist," then he could not desire the return of an "undifferentiated" social state. Logic prevents Wagner from holding both positions at the same time. But even if he held these positions at different times in his life, the disparity between the two views is so great that the student of the *Ring* receives little if any assistance from knowing Wagner's personal opinions. The references: Maurice Boucher, *The Political Concepts of Richard Wagner*, trans. Marcel Honoré (New York: M & H Publications, 1950), p. 180; Robert W. Gutman, *Richard Wagner: The Man, His Mind, and His Music* (New York: Harcourt, Brace & World, Inc., 1968), p. 119.

14. It is interesting to note in this regard that on the first page of his introduction (p. 13), Donington asserts: "No book could even begin to be adequate to the subject of Wagner's *Ring* which did not move on several levels at once, and perhaps the more the levels, the more adequate the book." Unfortunately, theory and practice are at odds, at least with respect to Donington's treatment of the symbolic significance of contracts. On those levels which he selects for analysis, Donington's achievement is quite extraordinary. The methodological objection raised above does not touch that achievement as it stands, but merely makes explicit a possible line of interpretation that Donington's critical conclusions tend to conceal.

15. Kurt Overhoff, *Wagners Niebelungen-Tetralogie* (Salzburg: Universitätsverlag Anton Pustet, 1971), p. 18. Italics in text.

Chapter 2. Contracts and Oaths in the *Ring*

1. Wagner explicitly omitted the definite article in titling the fourth and final music drama of the *Ring*, as the 1911 Breitkopf & Härtel edition of Wagner's complete works clearly indicates (6: 177). Thus, references should be to "*Götterdämmerung,*" not to "*Die Götterdämmerung.*" Apparently the purpose of this linguistic nicety was to suggest that "twilight of the gods" had a certain finality about it that "*the* twilight of the gods" lacked.

2. For example, in the second act of *Die Walküre*, Wotan is referred to as *Siegvater*, and in the second and third acts as *Walvater;* in the third act of *Siegfried*, he is referred to as *Streitvater.*

3. The secondary literature contains a number of divergent opinions on this matter. In the program for the 1965 Bayreuth Festival, Lynn Snook remarks in passing that the Rhinemaidens are "daughters of a demonic father. . . ." But there is no textual evidence (*a*) that the *Vater* is the actual congenital father of the Rhinemaidens (i.e., their reference could be to a "father" in a religious sense) and (*b*) that he is "demonic." Donington's observation is that "Wagner's Rhinemaidens, his Valkyries, his Norns are all members of the same family with different characteristics uppermost." But this is another claim in the Jungian spirit and is not helpful here. Although Wotan sired the Valkyries, he could hardly have been the father of the Rhinemaidens for the reasons given; thus, the real identity of the *Vater* and his precise relation to the Rhinemaidens remains unclear. Perhaps the final word on the subject is by Tibor Knief. On this point, his article-length study concludes: "Who this father may be is revealed neither from the conversation of the Rhinemaidens nor from the subsequent development of the plot." The references: Lynn Snook, "Rheingold, or the Power and Vainglory of the Gods," *Bayreuther Festspiele Programmhefte* 1965 (Bayreuth), p. 32; Donington, *Wagner's "Ring,"* p. 145; Tibor Knief, "Zur Deutung der Rheintöchter in Wagners *Ring,*" *Archiv für Musikwissenschaft* 26 (1969): 303.

4. This passage makes the distinction even more explicit. It reads:

> Hast du dem Rhein
> das Gold zum Ringe geraubt?
> Erzeugtest du gar
> den zähen Zauber im Reif?

> (Did you steal the gold
> for the ring from the Rhine?

Did you produce
the ring's alluring magic?)

5. For example, the Valkyrie Schwertleite mentions "Alberich's ring" (*Alberichs Reif*) at the beginning of the third act of *Die Walküre*. And in the prologue to *Götterdämmerung*, the staging refers to "Alberich's ring" (*Ring Alberichs*) as Siegfried draws it from his finger and gives it in pledge to Brünnhilde. Although Wagner's staging does not always designate the ring as Alberich's, the point is that in crucial situations (for instance, when it is changing hands) the ring *is* referred to as Alberich's long after Alberich himself has lost the ring to Wotan. Therefore, due credibility must be given to Alberich's continued right to possess the ring. In contrast, Kurt Overhoff claims that Brünnhilde "is and remains" the "only legitimate" possessor of the ring. However, I do not understand how this exclusive position can be maintained in view of Wagner's stage directions and also for the reasons given above. Overhoff appeals to Brünnhilde's "metaphysical right" to the ring but does not elucidate the metaphysics involved. See Overhoff, *Wagners Tetralogie*, p. 102.

6. Species of trees are variously differentiated in the *Ring*. Thus, Siegmund tells of an "oak tree" (*Eiche*) outside the house where he lived as a boy. Hunding's hut is dominated by a large ash tree, as noted above. During Siegfried's adventures in the second act of *Siegfried*, he periodically rests and lingers under a "linden tree" (*Linde*). And in the prologue to *Götterdämmerung*, the Norns tie the rope of fate to a "pine tree" (*Tanne*). The careful details of Wagner's staging are as relevant to the structure of thought in the *Ring* as they are to its purely visual and aesthetic dimension. Therefore, as an aside on the perennial problem of Wagnerian staging, the more details such as the different types of tree are sacrificed in the name of streamlining the *Ring's* "dated" realism, the less the visual symbolism can become a part of the *Ring's* philosophical dimension.

7. According to Shaw, we find Brünnhilde at this point "swearing a malicious lie to gratify her personal jealousy. . . ." (p. 77). But this judgment is hasty, and in fact reduces a complex interpersonal matter to a single emotional reaction. Does Brünnhilde "lie" when she claims that Siegfried has committed perjury? The answer is involved, but one can make a good case (as I shall attempt below) that the answer is no. And her swearing an oath in retaliation against Siegfried's supposed abuse of oaths need be no more "malicious" and the result of "personal jealousy" than Wotan's action against Siegmund when the latter violates the oath of marriage between Hunding and Sieglinde.

8. A passage from Wagner's letter to Roeckel may be cited here (quoted in Donington, *Wagner's "Ring,"* p. 148): "Thus the whole unfolding of the drama illustrates the need to recognize and accept the diversity, the perpetual changing, the eternal renewals of reality and of life."

Chapter 3. Retrospect

1. For a different approach to the relation between nature as such and human nature, see Theodor W. Adorno, *Versuch über Wagner* (Frankfurt am Main: Suhrkamp Taschenbuch, 1974), pp. 126–27.

2. For Newman's formulation of the problem, see the second volume of his Wagner biography, pp. 332–33. The reader will recall that this problem has already been discussed in a different context in chapter 1.

3. Nietzsche's remark in *"Der Fall Wagner"* is instructive. He connects the "trouble" (*Unheil*) which besets the old world with the "contracts" (*Verträgen*) on which that world rests. However, he does not develop the point here or elsewhere. See Nietzsche, *Werke*, 2: 910–11.

4. This information is contained in the initial stage directions for the prologue to *Götterdämmerung*. According to Wagner, the "first" (*erste*) Norn is the "oldest" (*älteste*). The second and third Norns are younger and youngest respectively. In *Das Rheingold*, Erda refers to the Norns, her daughters, as "primevally conceived" (*ur-erschaffne*). The student of *Ring* discrepancies might question how "primeval" beings can also be distinguished according to temporal (i.e., historical) differentiations. However, even if this potential discrepancy is a real problem, I do not believe that it significantly alters anything of substance in the plot.

Select Bibliography

The secondary literature on Wagner and his works is enormous. Although the entries listed below are few in number, they represent a solid core of scholarship from which the serious student may develop an understanding of the *Ring*.

Adorno, Theodor W. *Versuch über Wagner.* Frankfurt am Main: Suhrkamp, 1952. Reprint. Frankfurt am Main: Suhrkamp Taschenbuch, 1974.

Bertram, Johannes. *Mythos, Symbol, Idee in Richard Wagners Musik-Dramen.* Hamburg: Hamburger Kulterverlag, 1957.

Boucher, Maurice. *The Political Concepts of Richard Wagner.* Translated by Marcel Honoré. New York: M & H Publications, 1950.

DiGaetani, John Louis. *Penetrating Wagner's Ring; an Anthology.* Rutherford: Fairleigh Dickinson University Press, 1978.

Donington, Robert. *Wagner's "Ring" and Its Symbols.* 3d ed. New York: St. Martin's Press, 1974.

Gutman, Robert W. *Richard Wagner: The Man, His Mind, and His Music.* New York: Harcourt, Brace & World, Inc., 1968.

Hartmann, Otto Julius. *Die Esoterik im Werk Richard Wagners.* Freiburg i. Br.: Verlag Die Kommenden, 1960.

Hutcheson, Ernest. *A Musical Guide to the Ring of the Nibelungen.* New York: Simon and Schuster, 1940.

Knief, Tibor. "Zur Deutung der Rheintöchter in Wagners Ring." *Archiv für Musikwissenschaft* 26 (1969): 297–306.

Mann, Thomas. *Essays of Three Decades.* Translated by H. T. Lowe-Porter. New York: Alfred A. Knopf, 1947.

Newman, Ernest. *The Life of Richard Wagner.* 4 vols. London: Cassell, 1933–47.

———. *Wagner as Man and Artist.* New York: Random House, 1924.

Nietzsche, Friedrich. *Werke in Drei Bänden.* Edited by Karl Schlechta. Munich: Carl Hanser Verlag, 1966.

Overhoff, Kurt. *Wagners Nibelungen-Tetralogie*. Salzburg: Universitätsverlag Anton Pustet, 1971.

Rather, L. J. *The Dream of Self-Destruction: Wagner's Ring and the Modern World*. Baton Rouge: Louisiana State University Press, 1979.

Shaw, George Bernard. *The Perfect Wagnerite*. 4th ed., 1923. Reprint. New York: Dover, 1967.

Snook, Lynn. "Rheingold, or the Power and Vainglory of the Gods." *Bayreuther Festspiele Programmhefte:* Bayreuth, 1965.

Stein, Herbert von. *Dichtung und Musik im Werk Richard Wagners*. Berlin: Walter De Gruyter & Co., 1962.

Taylor, Ronald. *Richard Wagner His Life, Art and Thought*. New York: Taplinger Publishing Co., 1979.

Wagner, Richard. *Sämmtliche Schriften und Dichtungen*. 12 vols. Leipzig: Breitkopf & Härtel, 1911.

———. *Sein Leben in Briefen*. Edited by Carl Siegmund Benedict. Leipzig: Breitkopf & Härtel, 1913.

———. *Collected Prose Works*. 8 vols. Translated by W. A. Ellis. New York: Broude Brothers, 1892, 1899.

Weston, Jessie L. *The Legends of the Wagner Drama*. New York: Charles Scribner's Sons, 1900.

Index

Adorno, Theodor, 29, 129

Alberich: and contract for power, 65; curse of, 22, 63–66; and Hagen, 91–92, 123; as owner of ring, 112, 129; and renunciation of love, 59–62, 109; and Rhinemaidens, 58–60, 61; and right to ring, 66; and Wotan, 36, 58–67, 84

Art: and life, 20; and the *Ring*, 18

Ash tree, 35, 46, 78, 98, 101, 107–8, 110, 115

Bigamy, 53

Blood-brotherhood: oath of, 86–87

Brünnhilde: as divine, 80–81, 85, 97–98, 99–100; and freedom, 117–18; and love, 22–23; and oaths, 80–81; and Siegfried, 49, 79–85, 98; and Siegmund, 97; and warriors, 47; and wisdom, 81–83, 100, 115; as woman, 100; and Wotan, 46, 72, 97–98, 118

Contracts: and Alberich, 65; and giants, 41–42; institution of, 37–38, 39, 79, 95, 104–8; and Jungian psychology, 29–31; leitmotif for, 17, 22, 86; and loss of power, 58–101; and nature, 39, 57; and origin of power, 34–40; and preservation of power, 40–58; in redeemed world, 103–11; as source of evil, 34, 38, 46–47, 62–64, 79, 95, 104–8; universality of, 57–58

Cosmology: in *Ring*, 56, 57–58

Curse. *See* Alberich: curse of

Divinity: of Brünnhilde, 80–81, 85, 97–98, 99–100

Donington, Robert, 29–31, 127, 128, 129

Donner, 42, 117

Dragon: Fafner as, 69

Dwarves, 42, 58, 60, 66, 119

Erda: and freedom, 116–17; and prophecy to Wotan, 55; and wisdom, 55–57, 74, 92, 109, 113–14; and Wotan, 45, 50, 54–57, 73, 105, 123

Evil, 38; contracts as source of, 34, 38, 46–47, 62–64, 79, 95, 104–8

Fafner, 42, 84, 109, 113, 119, 121

Fasolt, 41, 42, 117, 119, 121

Fear: Siegfried and, 70, 79, 83; and symbolism of the ring, 31–32

Freedom: and Brünnhilde, 117–18; and dwarves, 119; and giants, 119; and nature, 120–21; and Rhinemaidens, 119–20; as value in redeemed world, 116–22; and Wotan, 47–54, 63, 73, 96, 117

Freia, 40–44, 48

Fricka, 42, 44, 45; and Wotan, 47–54, 63, 72, 74, 96, 117

Froh, 52, 62, 103

Giants, 40–45, 119

Gibichungs, 86–89

Gods: and dependence on contracts, 40–44, 48, 50–51; limited power of, 41, 73, 74, 104–6; origin of, 103–4

Gold: forging of ring from, 59, 109, 122; power of, 36–37, 59, 81, 110, 122; return of, 120; symbolism of, 22, 109; theft of, by Alberich, 59–60; theft of, by Wotan, 61–62

Grimheld, 123

Gunther: and Siegfried, 86–97, 109

Gutrune, 86, 89, 90, 93, 96

Hagen: and Alberich, 91–92; birth of, 123; as owner of ring, 93, 95–96, 109, 112–13; and plot against Brünnhilde, 86, 90, 95; and